Diary of a
High Maintenance Woman

Diary of a
High Maintenance Woman:
Love Lessons I Learned the Hard Way!

beth elias

Copyright © 2002 by Beth Elias.

Library of Congress Number: 2001119560
ISBN #:   Hardcover   1-4010-3850-6
                 Softcover   1-4010-3849-2

All rights reserved. No part of this book may be reproduced or transmitted in any form or by any means, electronic or mechanical, including photocopying, recording, or by any information storage and retrieval system, without permission in writing from the copyright owner.

This book was printed in the United States of America.

To order additional copies of this book, contact:
Xlibris Corporation
1-888-7-XLIBRIS
www.Xlibris.com
Orders@Xlibris.com

CONTENTS

Acknowledgements 9

Chapter 1
    "The History" 11

Chapter 2
    Lesson Number One
"Men and Women Really **ARE** from Different Planets!" 20

Chapter 3
    Lesson Number Two
"I **AM** a High Maintenance Woman . . . and That's OK!" 38

Chapter 4
    Lesson Number Three
"Live in the Reality, **NOT** the Fantasy" 52

Chapter 5
    Lesson Number Four
"Beware of the M.O.D.!" 65

Chapter Six
    Lesson Number Five
"Sex ≠ Love" 83

Chapter 7
    Lesson Number Six
Give Good "C" 96

Chapter 8
Lesson Number Seven
"Love DOESN'T Conquer All!" 109

Chapter 9
Lesson Number Eight
"There Is No 'Y' in Love" 123

Chapter 10
Lesson Number Nine
Breaking Up is HARD To Do! 134

Chapter 11
Lesson Number Ten
"Time is a 4-Letter Word" 148

Chapter 12
"The Wrap" 161

Acknowledgements

To My Cowboy, Mr. Porsche, The Exec, and Casper – Thanks to each of you for the many wonderful memories we shared. Thank you for having such an impact on my life. And thank you for helping me become the woman I am today! You will always have a piece of my heart!

To Mom & Dad – Thank you for giving me so much love and so many wonderful gifts. The confidence, drive, and sense of balance you provided have given me the power to fearlessly chase all my dreams! You are the best parents in the world! Love you bunches!

To my sisters B.J., Barb, and Bindy – Thank you for being the most amazing sisters! You each had a profound impact on my growth and I'm grateful that I have always had such wonderful examples to follow. I love you with muchness!

To my best friends in life Paige, Cheryl, and Nori – I can't imagine how I could have survived the last thirteen years without each of you. Thank you for listening until you thought you might explode. Thank you for trying to keep me out of bad relationships, even though it usually did not work. Thank you for always supporting my dreams. I love you and am so lucky to have your support and friendship!

To Harold – Thank you for supporting our family through the toughest of times. We are lucky you are part of the bunch! Thank you for performing my wedding ceremony . . . BOTH times! Love you!

Acknowledgements

To Terry – We're challenging, but worth it! I'm glad you are part of the family!

To Christina, Stacey, Jordan, and Justin – You are the best nieces and nephews an aunt could have. I'm very proud of each of you and hope you will always pursue your dreams. A great education gives you the coolest choices! Love you lots!

To Greg – My dearest of friends. I carry your memory with me always. You give me strength every day. You are my angel in heaven!

Thank you to the team at BDS Marketing for my fabulous cover and logo design!

Thanks to John Sweeney and the team at One Image for my fabulous cover photography!

Barb, Harold, Nori, and Allan – Special thanks for taking on the task of editing!

Chapter 1

"The History"

I think it's time for an official "man break". It's May 1999 and I am on a plane leaving Miami after a very painful week. I am in an emotional tug of war, a mix of many feelings . . . sad yet relieved, depressed but optimistic, stressed out yet strangely calm. Is it humanly possible to have this many competing emotions and live to tell about it? My entire life seems to be in chaos, every aspect unsettled. I am starting a new job, relocating to Chicago, a place I frequently compare to hell, and have just endured the disastrous finale of a relationship I thought might be the happy ending to this book. So here I sit on this plane, unable to keep the tears from rolling down my face. I try to brush them away quickly so people won't feel sorry for me . . . I just hate feeling pitied. The past several years have certainly presented me with an overload of life's little challenges!

Welcome to my world. I'm the kind of girl most of you love to hate. From the surface, I appear to have it all . . . a killer career with a six digit salary, great health with enough energy for ten people, and a 5'2" petite blonde exterior that still lets me stop traffic on a good hair day. At 34, at least I recognize what a blessed young lady I am. My parents are incredible and are the reason I have been able to enjoy some amazing life situations while keeping my feet firmly planted on the ground. My three older sisters have all given me many gifts in life and I feel lucky to reflect a little of each of them in my personality. I am fortunate to have many deep friendships that have lasted almost my entire span of life. I have a great education, completed my undergraduate degree in three years, graduated first in my marketing class, held a 4.0 in my major, and managed to do it all while I was a Dallas Cowboys Cheerleader. I completed my master's degree the following year and shortly landed a great job at a large communications company. My career has provided me with exciting trips to Singapore, Budapest, London, Mexico, Hong Kong, France, and, of course, all over the U. S. It is safe to say that I have already experienced a lifetime of opportunities most people only dream about.

Sounds like a charmed life, don't you think? So why am I feeling so worthless as I sit here on this plane, headed to tackle my latest and greatest life adventure? Why do I feel as though no man will ever want to be in a relationship with me, that I am somehow a defective female? How can I possibly be feeling sorry for myself? Because I am a "high maintenance" woman. And damn proud of it, because I have worked hard to earn that title! It took a great deal of learning about myself to recognize that I am high maintenance. And I had to learn not only about myself, but about women in general, about men, about relationships, and about life before I could really understand what high maintenance means. It is a term that used to make the hair on the back of my neck stand up. But after reflecting on all my life experiences, I can tell you now that I wouldn't have it any other way! You see, high maintenance is NOT a bad thing. Keep reading and you will soon understand why.

Perhaps it is already obvious to you that despite my list of "accomplishments", I have managed continuous failure in one area. MEN. Four failed long term relationships . . . my relationship with a high school boyfriend I'll call "My Cowboy" lasted seven years, with my first husband "Mr. Porsche", five years, with my second husband "The Exec", six years, and now "Casper", my "affair of the heart" for well over a year . . . he is just not going to be the happy ending I hoped for! After eight successful years at a "male dominated" company, you would think I'd have been around men enough to master an understanding of the opposite sex. After all, I work with men, negotiate with men, manage men, and befriend men every day. I've known all kinds of men, executives, engineers, salesmen, teachers, athletes, you name it. So why do I seem to interface with them successfully in any situation except an intimate relationship? Why do I find myself continuously nursing a broken heart? I am not alone here. Why do you think there is a never ending stream of relationship books hitting the shelves? If it is so easy to have a lasting relationship, why is the divorce rate approaching 60% in our country? What's the deal when an intelligent, friendly, attractive new age woman cannot be successful in a relationship? IS SOMETHING WRONG WITH ME? When I couldn't answer this question, I went on a total self-exploration trip.

In this book, I'm going to take you through my little journey of discovery that helped me realize that I am indeed a high maintenance woman. I'll also explain my definition of high maintenance and share ten important life lessons I learned while on my self-exploration trip. And I'm writing this book to kill two birds with one stone ... to help myself deal with these lessons and to help you learn them before you have to experience the same kind of pain! Ladies, think of me as the one friend who will tell you the truth, even the stuff you didn't really want to hear. Guys, think of me as that one friend you seek when you must have a woman's opinion. I am about to share my life secrets with you, to give you my pure chick perspective. So listen closely, and perhaps you will keep from finding this stuff out THE HARD WAY!

I think it's important to share with you a little of my *relationship hell* history to insure that we are all on the same page as we review these lessons. Let's start with the summary version of my relationship meltdowns. I met My Cowboy at the end of my freshman year of high school on a church trip. The first love of my life, I have to admit this was actually one of the most mature relationships I have ever experienced. We were best friends. He was the quarterback of his high school football team. I was the captain of my drill team. Although we went to different high schools, we were as close as two people could be on every level. Somehow we managed to stay above things like jealousy and pettiness. I think our core strength was the fact that we were truly best friends. In fact, I'd say our ability to communicate was uncanny for our age. But then we went on to separate colleges. He moved to Texas A&M three hours south of Dallas, where I stayed to cheer for the Cowboys and attend UTA. For him, it was the perfect of situations, a girlfriend at home, freedom at school. For me, it was my first of many exercises in loneliness. I wrote him every day and tried to see him as much as possible. During those three years, I did a lot of growing up, and we did a lot of growing apart. When I went down to A&M to complete my master's degree, it seemed I was crowding his space. Honestly, I think we were just at different life stages. I was ready for things to grow more serious and become engaged, but he was fearful of taking things to that kind of level. He just wasn't sure I was the girl with whom he could spend the rest of his life. I couldn't understand how you could be with someone for seven years and not know if you wanted to take things to the next level, even at that young age. We eventually split. It was as painful as a divorce for us both. I attempted to do a little dating during the process, but I learned I was a relationship girl, and "playing the field" was something that I didn't really enjoy.

Immediately I began to date Mr. Porsche. Friends from high school, we dated while both attending Texas A&M for about nine months. When I completed my degree, I went back to Dallas to work while he stayed down at school to finish his degree. We were married upon his graduation that May, after only dating a year and a half, and spending only those first nine months in the same city. We were completely wrong for each other, but too young to recognize it at the time. I think there should be a law that prohibits marriage until you hit 30! I guess we were just looking for different things out of life and out of marriage. He was looking for "Susie HomeMaker", however, I was "Carrie CareerChick". He thought my career drive was great while we were dating, but not so hot once I became his wife. We spent very little time together. He was starting his own business while managing a full time job, and spent every night in our garage making custom design parts for race cars. My second period of great loneliness, I felt neglected and depressed. It was never the kind of relationship I needed. I'm sure I wasn't giving him what he needed either. But it was so important to me to make my marriage "work". So despite the fact that I was unhappy within the first six months, I stayed in a very painful marriage for three years. I think I was in love with the concept of love. In fact, I probably still am in love with the concept. And I did love him. Those feelings were very strong, and it was quite hard for me to end my marriage. But it was absolutely the right move. I moved in and out of our house four times before I was gone for good. We went to marriage counseling. I was struggling with so many things. It took another four months to actually do the paperwork. And then things got really ugly, and I can honestly say we both behaved horribly while going through the divorce process. I think it is so sad that divorce can bring out the worst in two really great people.

During that split, I began to date The Exec. Although we lived in different states, we had become close friends at work. I do not think I would have ever managed to become strong enough to leave Mr. Porsche if I did not have The Exec to support me. He was ready for our relationship to grow beyond friendship long before I was and pursued me like no one ever had before. The first time I flew to Denver to spend the weekend with him, he picked me up at the airport in a limousine, had roses in the car, champagne for himself, and a Dr. Pepper for me. (My addiction to Dr. Pepper is legendary . . . he knew I would prefer it to champagne!) At any rate, the entire period we dated was like a whirlwind. He literally swept me off my feet. While we were dating, never once did I arrive at an airport without flowers waiting for me at the other end. We spent hours on the phone every day. Being away from him was terribly difficult. The potential of our relationship seemed just boundless. He took me on a surprise trip to Hawaii to ask me to be his wife. The Exec was energetic, charismatic, very intelligent, extremely driven. I felt we had so much in common. I loved him so deeply. I felt certain that I had found my life partner. The fall of this relationship is quite a long story, and I will save the detail of its crash for primary examples of how I learned many of my hard lessons. Basically he decided being married to me caused him to make compromises he really did not want to make. But when he told me he wanted a divorce, I was completely unprepared. I was totally clueless, completely heartbroken. I spent an entire year trying to convince him to change his mind, of course to no avail, and to much extended pain for myself. I felt as though my life would never be the same.

Enter the picture Casper. I was never more vulnerable. We met in our builder's office as we were both under new home construction in the same city. We found we had several mutual friends. A few days after we met, he sent me a friendly e-mail. I responded in the most neighborly sort of way. And then we got a little flirty. And then we got a little deep. And then we built something that felt truly amazing over e-mail. The first time he kissed me, I went completely dizzy and actually lost my balance. I thought perhaps he was my soul mate. He told me he thought it was fate. Finally I felt like my split with The Exec might not have been meaningless after all. Casper explained that his girlfriend of many years, we'll call her "Snow White" because she seemed so naïve and sweet, was going to be moving in with her mother when he moved into his house. He described his love for her as that of a father for a child. She was almost ten years younger than him, and while it was apparent that he loved her very much, he indicated there was just too much missing in their relationship for it to continue. Again, I'm saving the details, but he told me for an entire year that he was going to leave her before anything but many passionate kisses, lots of coffee stops, and a stream of memorable e-mail passed between us. Every time I mentally questioned what was going on, I was able to justify his every action because of my own internal struggles ending my past relationships. As luck would have it, we both began traveling to the same city on business, and our relationship then blossomed into much more than a flirty friendship. For seven months, we had quite an affair, with many ups and downs, including this current move of mine to Chicago. Three months into it, I attempted to bring the relationship to a screeching halt because he proposed to Snow White over Christmas. However, he explained that a counselor had convinced him his issue was "fear of commitment". He felt if he didn't take that step, he would never know whether or not it was his fault, that he needed to do everything possible to make it work. I remembered feeling exactly the same thing when I left Mr. Porsche. My solution was marriage counseling to insure that I had personally taken every step. Casper swore the engagement was a mistake he planned to correct, and I believed him. He broke the engagement before a business trip to Europe three months later, and I joined him for an amazing five days. When we returned to our respective cities, he couldn't stay away from Snow White. They reconciled. Again, I was completely devastated.

Fast forward with me, it's now September 2001, and I'm a several months into recovery from yet another brief round with Casper. He was in and out of my life so many times I have completely lost count! Over the past three years, we approached something that never quite materialized into a full-blown relationship. It has been very difficult for me to move on alone, but I know that it is the right thing to do. And all this pain would be the reason that throughout the two years I've been writing this book, I've been on my "official man break".

It is hard for me to even look at couples together now. My heart just feels so empty. I know that only time will help this pass, and I am grateful that I had the opportunity for so much love already in my life. Many people never experience love even once, and I have already enjoyed four great loves! Often, I find myself wondering if perhaps I am just so blessed in other areas of my life that relationship success may be unachievable for me. I have learned that I am overly trusting and way too forgiving in my relationships . . . gifts my father gave to me. But I prefer this combination to being incapable of trust and forgiveness. Finding a happy medium on the scale between unconditional trust and none at all would probably be a great self-improvement activity for me. But, hey, then I wouldn't be me! At least I am now able to recognize my own deficiencies and make conscious decisions while keeping them in perspective. And I give a lot of credit to The Exec and to Casper, because they both made me think about what was really important to me. That drove me to actually write this book! Nothing wrong with a little motivation to sit down, reflect on the past, and learn from those mistakes!

Enough background, time to dive into the details. I'm going to share ten lessons with you in this book, lessons I unfortunately had to learn the hard way! They are:

#1 – Men & women really ARE from different planets!
#2 – I AM a high maintenance woman . . . and that's OK!
#3 – Live in the reality, NOT the fantasy!
#4 – Beware of the M.O.D.!
#5 – Sex ≠ Love!
#6 – Give Good "C"!
#7 – Love DOESN'T conquer all!
#8 – There is no "Y" in love!
#9 – Breaking up is HARD to do!
#10 – Time is a 4-letter word!

So, let's take a look at those lessons one by one, and see if perhaps I can motivate you to avoid the pitfalls that have entrapped me. Throughout this book, I'll use some examples from my first three failed relationships to emphasize the lessons. And you will actually ride with me on the Casper roller coaster, experiencing the emotions, the pain, and several lessons as I learn them myself! Remember that I'm only giving you one side of the story here. I think My Cowboy, Mr. Porsche, The Exec, and Casper are all super guys and I had some wonderful memories with each of them.

But I'm giving you lots of examples of things that went wrong with my relationships because these events were the catalysts for me to learn these lessons. So before you give in to the temptation to rush to judgment about any of these guys or about me, remember that you are only getting a snapshot of information from a few specific moments. I challenge you to keep an open mind! I'm just sharing my life experiences with you to make you stop and think about your own actions. I'm not a professional and I don't have any magic answers. This is just my own chick perspective. Enjoy!

Chapter 2

Lesson Number One

"Men and Women Really **ARE** from Different Planets!"

I thank The Exec, ex-hubby #2, for teaching me my first lesson the hard way. I guess I had probably learned others before this one, but this was the first lesson I consciously recognized while I was learning it! Call it my first "ah ha!" Very simply, I realized that men and women are different. Ok, I know it sounds very cliché. But it is so completely true. In fact, you are probably plagued by it just a bit each day without even recognizing it. So let me be the one to hit you over the head with the baseball bat and wake you up. The basis for understanding myself and preparing to do things differently in my future relationships came from studying men and women and understanding that, indeed, we are just *different*.

It was August 1996 when The Exec, whom at the time I truly believed to be the love of my life, told me he wanted a divorce. I spent a year in mourning, but also "in research". I wanted to understand why on earth he felt compelled to quit on our relationship. How could someone with whom I was deeply in love need so badly to be away from me? Was there anything I could possibly change about myself to make him want to stay with me? I read every book I could get my hands on about relationships. I went through three books in John Gray's Venus and Mars series, two by relationship expert Barbara DeAngelis, several books by various men about "what they want" . . . oh the list was long but distinguished. I watched television programs that were focused on relationships. I paid close attention to the behavior of every man in my life. I took away parts of business training programs that were applicable to personal relationships. And I also saw a counselor. Then I took all this learning and reflected. And analyzed. And questioned. And understood. Then summarized those lessons – lucky you.

Many things became completely obvious to me once I realized that men and women are not the same. People are all different. DUH. Men and women are particularly different. DUH. This is the first thing we all have to accept if we are to be successful in our relationships. Why do we continue to fight this fact? Accept it, my friends, and you will feel as though you have had a revelation. I promise that if you just remember no one is just like you, your gift will be a more flexible point of view. No one is going to think, react, or behave just like you. And when you expect your partner to just automatically understand you and your thought process, you are forgetting that no one thinks, reacts, or behaves just like you. That creates problems. Likewise, if you don't take the time to truly understand your mate, you run the risk of creating additional problems because you will find yourself making incorrect assumptions. Tragic, but most of us are guilty. And it's probably why so many of us spend a lot of time feeling misunderstood.

The simple reality is that women and men use different processes to think, feel, and communicate. And let's be clear, I don't want to stereotype. I'm not going to tell you that this is concrete, that this is your list of differences, learn it and you will succeed. Nope, it's just a few high level things that appear to be pretty consistent if you are able to sift through all the technical opinions and information from "experts". In fact, you will probably see many of these things reflected by folks you know. It is so important that you remember every person is different. That means these characteristics will vary from person to person. And while I am sharing things that appear to be typically more "male" behavior or more "female" behavior, realize that both men and women are both capable of any of these behaviors. In fact, I can see that I am more "male" in some of my processes, and I know this helps me to be successful in my business dealings with men. The trick is learning to make these differences work for your relationship instead of against your relationship. Now that I understand these simple concepts, I am already more successful in my job, more understanding in my friendships, and able to handle relationship issues in a way that I was not capable of before. And remember, this is just my chick perspective. I'm just sharing with you the things I've learned myself. These are sincerely my own opinions . . . there's no wrong or right here. I'm just hoping to make you stop and think! But you are the only one who can determine what works for you!

So let's look at some of the key differences I think I've seen. First and foremost, it seems men and women have a critical difference on the issue of sex. Ladies, I hate to break this news to you, but guys do not feel the same way we do about sex. You can spend the next four chapters in denial, but this difference is so huge and so important that I have dedicated an entire chapter to the topic! (see lesson #5, Sex ≠ Love!) But there are other key differences, less obvious ones that impact how we interact with each other every day, and I have a short list of those that I've lovingly nicknamed the "big three". In fact, I think if you can just grasp the big three, you will be on your way to immediately enhancing the relationships in your life, whether they are friendships, business partnerships, or intimate relationships. So let's start by just defining these three key differences. It is very important that they are clear. I promise I will try to remind you of these differences throughout the rest of the chapters. And I will also point out lots of painful personal experiences to help you relate to what I'm talking about. So let's jump right into the big three.

Big difference number one: Our focus in life is different. It seems that men typically focus on the results, while women typically focus on the process. Too vague, do you need a translation? Men desire to get straight to the point. They are on a mission, filtering through any information that doesn't get them straight to the end result. They are forcefully determined to find a solution to whatever problem faces them at the moment. Women are taking in the "big picture" along the way. We look at all factors that are influencing whatever is going on, and notice things that don't necessarily have to do with the end result. Let me put this philosophical stuff into a practical example for you. Have you ever tried to have a conversation with a guy when he's just returned from the store with any piece of electronic equipment? He must immediately connect whatever it is, hook up the new stereo, set up the Nintendo, whatever. It requires his undivided attention. It's a new problem to be solved . . . a goal driven by the ultimate result of a new functional electronic toy. Hey, he doesn't even stop to read those directions!!! He just dives right in, ignoring anything else going on around him until his new toy is functional.

But for women, it's more about the process than the result. For example, just look at the way we shop. It is often simply about the experience of heading to the mall, looking in all the stores, trying on a number of outfits we find interesting, looking at everything from lipstick to cookware, perhaps returning home completely empty handed. Ok, maybe not completely empty-handed! But when we return from the spree, we want to share the process, we want to talk about our search for the perfect outfit, how we found great sales, how we saved so much money, all the great things we saw that weren't even on our shopping plan. Is this difference starting to become clear? I sense this is also the defining trait that creates many behaviors we think are "typically" male. This might be the reason many guys are task-oriented. They are focused on one thing at a time. They do not watch football on TV and have conversation simultaneously. Their focus is on solving the problem at hand, one problem at a time. Women, on the other hand, are multitaskers. Any of you ladies cook dinner, do laundry, watch the baby, and talk on the phone at the same time today?

Big difference number two: Our key internal drivers are different. Men appear to be driven by accomplishment, women by relationships. Don't get bent out of shape ladies, I'm not saying that relationships are not important to men. But what I am telling you is that it seems that feeling of making something happen, that feeling of the win, that feeling of closing the deal, that responsibility of being the "bread winner", this is the core driver for many guys. And since we already understand that men are typically results oriented, this makes even more sense. This is probably the reason that to many men, the job is so critically important. Because frequently it is from his job that your man gets that sense of accomplishment fulfilled. In fact, I know many men who must have their career headed down the path they want before they can be successful in any other area of their lives. And if their careers are not where they want them to be, the rest of their lives go on hold until they fix the job front. So ladies, don't feel threatened by your guy's job. It's not that the job is more important than you. It's just that the job is critically important in a different way . . . it's one of the things that defines who he is. It is not something you have to compete with, and you will run into trouble if you spend each day expecting him to prove that you are more important than his job. Trust me when I tell you that in the big picture, you are more important. So try and be flexible enough to recognize he needs to do the right things at work to be successful. Recognize this fact and I promise you will rest easier every night. I would venture to guess this core driver of accomplishment is why men "chase" so well during those beginning phases of dating, and have such a change of behavior once we are "caught". Before we are caught, we are a challenge, a conquest waiting to happen. Once we are caught, mission accomplished, move on to the next opportunity for a win and that rush that goes with it! And when I say next opportunity,

I don't mean the next girl, I mean the next task! My gut also says this is the reason why many men have a difficult time having romantic relationships with highly successful business women. It's almost against their natural instinct to not be the "accomplisher" of the family.

For many women, however, relationships are the way in which we get our ultimate fulfillment. And I don't mean just that one special intimate relationship. I'm talking about all of them . . . the relationships we share with our friends, with our family, with our co-workers. We spend extensive time communicating, nurturing the bonds we have created, getting that sense of sharing that makes us feel connected and involved in life. We want to talk. We want to know what's going on in the lives of the people that are important to us. We want the opinions of those people. We want to know how they feel. We want to tell them about the details of our lives. So guys, don't feel concerned about the time we spend talking to our girlfriends and how much information we share. Believe me, we are going to tell our closest girlfriends things we'd expect you to take to the grave! Talking openly is just something that we do. It's something that defines us just like your job defines you . . . trust me when I tell you our girlfriends are NOT more important than you! But these relationships are essential for women. Communicating with those we are close to is part of what makes us tick. Don't feel threatened by this closeness we have to others, and please don't try to isolate us from others we are close to. I promise, our most important relationship is the one with our honey!

Here are some questions you can ask yourselves to help you further grasp this key difference in our internal drivers. Guys when you talk about work, do you talk about the projects, the deals, the wins? Ladies, when you talk about work, do you tend to talk about the people, your co-workers, your boss, the customers? Can you sense where your individual priorities lie? This difference in our key drivers also seems to be the one that makes many guys so competitive. I learned in all those books that most men HATE to be wrong. (Can you BELIEVE I actually had to do research to learn that?) And many men seem to think anyone who has a different opinion is saying, "You are wrong." Hey, I like to have my own perspective, and I certainly wouldn't assume that a person thought I was wrong just because their point of view was different than mine. Maybe that's because women seek out many opinions while fulfilling our relationship driver. So I was oblivious to the fact that when my opinions were different, I was often making the guys in my life feel "questioned". And since I'm not the kind of girl that just agrees with everything out of any guy's mouth just to keep the peace, I'm haunted by this factor both inside and outside my personal relationships. I even see it cause some issues with the men I talk to frequently at work. However, in the office, it appears guys are more open to other points of view than at home. (At least the ones who see me as a colleague first and a woman second . . . and that's a tragic few, but a different book!) I guess home is not a place guys want to feel questioned!

This difference in key internal drivers was a major contributor to the fall of my second marriage. The Exec and I used to go to verbal war over the most ridiculous issues, like whether or not the new marketing strategy for "company X" would work, and all because it was so important to him to win. And I could never just listen without having my own opinion. I could never just say, "Honey you are right. You are so brilliant." When my opinions were different than his on any business issue, he'd have to fight me on it. If I just said, "This doesn't really matter. Let's not argue over something unimportant," to attempt to shut down the heated discussion, that wasn't acceptable. It wasn't ok because he had to win to be right, and I had to concede defeat to make that happen. Of course, that wasn't something I did very often, primarily because I had no clue this was what was going on. Ahhhhhhhh, the beauty of hindsight! I think since women are more capable of seeing the big picture and recognizing that there are multiple ways to solve a problem, we don't feel that alternate opinions mean ours aren't just as valid. So we are clueless to the fact that it is a very big deal for our man to feel challenged, especially by the one person who should always be his number one ally, and that we make him feel challenged by expressing an opinion that is different than his. And if we ladies recognize this fact, it will help us improve our most important relationship, and OUR key driver.

Big difference number three: Our information processing techniques are different. Men tend to be more rational and analytical while women tend to be more intuitive and emotional. Here's an easy example. Guys, how long has it been since you've picked up the directions to anything? In general, guys will tackle any task without reading directions. Men use their analytical process to "figure out" what needs to happen, step by step. Men converse by focusing on the literal, the facts, the information. Women, however, tend to sense the emotions behind the actions. We pay close attention to interactions between people. We notice when someone is troubled and are very emotionally perceptive. How many times have you ladies been able to look at someone you are close to and just know that something isn't right? How many times have you been disappointed because your guy didn't "just know" something was wrong with you? Many women react with emotion, even to facts, because we are influenced by that big picture and all those outside factors. Guys generally don't react with emotion, because it's just information to them, and they are screening out everything but those key details. This is probably why sometimes we think you guys are "cold", because you are simply processing facts, and we can't understand why those facts don't cause a reaction!

The difference in the way we process information tends to become crystal clear during any kind of disagreement. Guys, do you get frustrated by women when we are "emotional" rather than "logical"? Do you feel like your girlfriend isn't making any sense when she is upset? Ladies, do you get frustrated because you are not being "heard", because your man cannot just "listen"? Women want their men to understand how they "feel". But feelings frequently defy logic and reason. And hence we have a big disconnect. When we are upset, our guy tries to solve the problem. If I said to The Exec, "I never see you any more," he would spout out the two times we actually did something together that month. He would have a counter for each point that came out of my mouth. But I was not looking for a solution, or for verification of my facts. I just wanted him to listen, to understand, to recognize that I missed him, and to give me a hug. Most guys will listen to the exact literal words, rather than sensing the overall emotion we are trying to communicate. So if we toss out things like, "I feel like I want to die," or "I can't live without you," they actually think we might be contemplating suicide.

While guys are busy using their logic to solve our problem of the moment, we are focused on the big picture and are hurt that they just "don't understand". Doesn't it seem that guys get really frustrated when we cry? I would watch The Exec getting angry with me when I was crying and I would just try so hard to understand what was frustrating him. After all, I was the one who was hurt and upset, why did that make HIM mad? It was simple. He felt responsible for me and for making me happy. When I was sad, he felt it was his fault . . . and that meant he did something "wrong". He was frustrated if he couldn't fix whatever was causing me to be upset. He just used his analytical process to try and solve my problem during the discussion. When it didn't work, he became angry. What a vicious cycle! But hey, this is also the gift that allows most men to fix everything they touch. Whether it's the checkbook that cannot be balanced no matter what, that rattle in the car, or that VCR we could not program to tape a favorite soap opera, guys use their analytical process to work their way through each and every situation. In fact, all of the big three differences can have benefits, and those are the points we must remember when we are trying to use these differences as enhancements to our relationships. Of course, we'll get into that discussion later in the book.

Ok, now that you have grasped the basics of the big three, let's look a bit more at how these key differences are at work creating havoc in our everyday interactions with members of the opposite sex. Realize that the big three insure that we think differently, communicate differently, and react differently. I'll give you a situation that used to happen to me all the time when The Exec and I were married. He would frequently travel overseas on business. In fact, we both traveled frequently, just to opposite sides of the globe most of the time! At any rate, when we first began to date, we lived in different states. He would call me every day without fail. We spent many hours on the phone. I think when you have a long distance relationship, you either learn to communicate effectively about everything, or you have nothing. He put tremendous energy into our relationship while we were dating... of course he was driven by accomplishing the "win". We actually had a little rule that said no matter what, we would always find time to talk every day. When we got married, however, we failed to make that rule continue to work. Here's how things would typically go. The Exec would hop a plane to Asia and, in the results-oriented male fashion, he would be completely focused on the end result of the trip. Actually, before he even left, he would be completely focused on whatever was happening at the office to get ready for the trip. In my typically female manner, I would be focused on the big picture. I would get sad, realizing that we were going to be apart for ten days. I would expect him to reserve some special time before he left. But I did not recognize that he had a completely different point of view. I would be disappointed that he didn't set aside that time for us to be together... because of course I expected his perspective to be just like mine. I interpreted his lack of attention as "he doesn't care".

Once on his trip, he would be out late with his colleagues discussing points of the day and setting strategy for the next meeting. The trips would be whirlwind. I was lucky to get a "hello" call between the meetings and dinner, and frequently the "social bonding" would keep the team out into the middle of the night. I would again be disappointed, hurt that I didn't "rate" enough for him to want to call. It was never an issue of trust for me. I wasn't worried that he was out with some other girl. It was simply that I felt so unimportant to him. How can you possibly feel important when you aren't an active part of your partner's life? And it got worse when he came home and had a million things that required his attention other than me. It was so different than the way he treated me when we were dating.

What I recognize now is simply that I was the project of his focus during the "chase", and once I was caught, I was not. I was "always going to be there" . . . so the other life issues just became the things that required his immediate attention. It really did not mean I wasn't important . . . he was just focusing on his goals and his priorities. He was responding to his key driver of "accomplishment" and was focusing on the next target to achieve his goals each day. And his analytical process, driven by logic, insured that he could not understand the emotional drivers causing me to be upset. I began to realize that if you can't recognize the differences in what makes you each tick and make an effort to work out ways to work around those differences, the relationship is going to fall apart. Let's be realistic, relationships are the key driver for many women. We'll never be happy unless we find a way to fulfill our relationship needs while enabling our guys to fulfill their accomplishment driver. And these things don't have to be mutually exclusive! The Exec wasn't doing anything wrong at all. He was just living life his way. When he would return, I would be upset and would make him feel as though he had done something wrong . . . because he wasn't doing what I wanted him to do. Self-fulfilling prophecy, the more upset I got, the less he wanted to be around me. Now I just recognize we had very different priorities, and I thought I was smart enough the next time to pick someone whose priorities were more similar to mine. That was Casper of course, but more on him later.

As I started to recognize the many differences between men and women, I began wondering how on earth a relationship can work with the opposite sex! Honestly, on the surface, it appears that it could be impossible to relate with any degree of success. And that's when I realized I needed to understand myself well enough to know which things are really important to me, and which things I can recognize as "guy things", and let them go. I have several friends who don't agree with this perspective. They think I am just making excuses for a guy to treat me badly, that I am "settling". But I keep saying to myself, "Thou shalt not judge," and I sincerely believe that is the right way to handle a relationship. In fact, I believe I used to be a very judgmental person and it took a lot of work for me to stop being such a tough critic. (See lesson #2 "I AM a High Maintenance Woman . . . and That's OK!") A relationship has to be give and take. There is no right and wrong. Isn't it almost impossible to remember that? I think the way you can make it work is to recognize what is important to you, and then find someone who has a similar life perspective. Ladies, I hate to break it to you, but it isn't our responsibility to find a guy with potential and then try and "fix" him. Guys, how many of you feel that your girl is always trying to change you? Girls, we must accept our man for what he is. It's funny how so many women expect to change their guy but are not at all open to changing themselves. If he isn't what you want when you find him, he isn't going to magically morph into it. A close friend often reminds me you shouldn't fall in love with someone's potential because he/she may never take advantage of it. It is very easy to fall into this trap because no one is perfect. But what you have to remember is that someone IS probably PERFECT FOR YOU. In my opinion, you "settle" when you stay with the person that needs dramatic change to be a fit for you. You deserve someone who makes you happy naturally.

The most successful relationships I see are the couples who have a great match of personalities, those who generally enjoy being around each other. Look, no one deserves to be your "improvement project". We each need to be our own person and live a happy life in that form. I know, it's really easy to write this sappy stuff and much harder to live it in real life. Trust me . . . four failed relationships and a novel's worth of pain . . . I know how hard! But that is why I say it is critical to find someone who thinks the same things in life are important. Pick your partner like you pick your friends. Choose someone you really just enjoy spending time with, and add the requirement of some major chemistry! Stay focused on those big important things, then recognize that when you believe in the same things, almost everything else is really about your "relationship process". And this thing I call the relationship process is really about how you recognize these differences we've already highlighted, then learn to work with them to enhance your relationship instead of allowing them to tear it apart. Remember, no relationship will be free from issues, but what makes or breaks it in the long run is how you handle those issues.

Now let me add some short rules to follow in addition to the big three differences. Ladies, I'm going to give you five rules to follow to keep your guy happy. Guys, I'm going to give you five rules that will make life easier with your girl. Let's start with the rules my fellow females need to follow.

1) Don't help him drive. Why is it that we feel compelled to help our guy operate his motor vehicle? Doesn't he have a license? Isn't he an adult, fully capable of driving in our absence? Yes to all of the above, so let him drive in peace. Do you need him to help you drive? No. So show him that you trust him to get you safely from point A to point B, and focus on something other than acting as his personal driving coach.

2) Don't analyze your relationship every day. Your relationship should be something you experience and enjoy. Lighten up on the daily assessment and try to avoid "talking" about it all the time. Spend your time together doing fun things. Honestly, no relationship is perfect, and most cannot live up to scrutiny on a daily basis. If you look for issues, believe me, you will find them and create problems. Don't spend each day judging how your honey reacts to every statement you make.

Your poor guy cannot live in an environment where he feels something is wrong all the time.

3) Don't stop turning him on. I mean it, girls. We have to just step up to the plate on this one and make a commitment to drive our men crazy all the time. It keeps the relationship charged. It will keep things interesting. If we want our guys to pay attention to us, we need to stay flirty and fun so he knows we find him sexy. Face it, sex is really important to men . . . see lesson #5! Pay attention to all those little things just like you did on day one of your relationship. I promise this will keep you connected like you couldn't imagine!

4) Let him do his "thing" in peace. All guys have it, the thing they like to do on their own. Maybe it's watch the football game, maybe it's golf, maybe it's tinker in the garage. Don't beat him up because he has a hobby he enjoys. You are not in competition with an activity. Golf does not bring the same kind of pleasure to his life that you do, and you don't need his attention twenty-four hours a day to have a great relationship. Give him some time to do his guy thing. After all, you don't want him to fight with you about your shopping time.

5) Let him be your big strong man. Hey all you women of the new millenium, as progressive as we like to think we are, guys still want to take care of us. LET your guy take care of you to some degree. It's one of his ways he shows he loves you. Don't get upset with him because he's trying to be your knight in shining armor . . . really, he knows you can do things by yourself, and he's not insinuating that you are not capable. He's not implying that you aren't wickedly intelligent. He just wants to lift the heavy things, pay the bills, and worry about the big stuff because it's how he shows love. Women are very verbal. We say the words "I love you", but guys

show love by trying to take care of us. It's a bit more subtle. So just relax a little and be thankful that you have someone sweet enough to want to help you! And when you honestly want to do it by yourself, be sweet back and give him another opportunity to help you. Say, "Why thank you so much for your help honey, but I've got this one . . . Could you help me with____ instead?"

Ok guys, your turn. Here are five rules you can follow to keep us girls glowing every day.

1) Call us if you are going to be late. Come on guys, for any appointment that you have during the work day, you would be kind enough to notify that person if you were going to be late. Can you say, "Cell phone?" Please show us the same respect. We can plan accordingly if we know you are going to be late in any situation. I know this can make you feel like you have a "keeper", but honestly, it's just a courtesy. If you don't let us know what's happening, we have to just let our imagination wander away until we hear from you. And of course, it's usually wandering in all the worst possible directions! Gentleman, how hard is it to pick up the phone, really?

2) Make time for us once a week. Anything at all, take us out for dinner. Take us to a movie. Take us for a drive. It doesn't have to be a big thing. You want us to desire you madly and rip your clothes off frequently? Keep dating us. Once a week, regardless of all those work things you have to do, spend time with us. Guys, I'm not kidding . . . consider this your insurance policy to get laid at least once a week. Hey, remember when you first started dating you would do anything to get that girl to say yes to a date? Don't let that perspective go. It's

pretty simple. If we don't spend time together, our connections grow weaker. When you ask us out, we know we are an important aspect of your life. We feel special, so we get excited. One thing each week, either pick one night that's sacred, or mix it up, but don't forget to do it. Consider it part of being our "big strong man" . . . ask us out even when we've been married for 30 years.

3) Listen just a little bit each day. Remember how we girls are all about relationships and bonding? We need to share with you . . . it's a girl thing. Talking is part of who we are. So just take a little time each day to listen. You do have ears for a more important reason than balancing your face. Please don't try and solve every problem. You don't need to do anything at all except listen. Please just hear what we are saying, and listen just because you know it is important to us. If we've had a bad day, just listen, then give us a hug and tell us it will be ok. This isn't rocket science, it's just a way that you can let us know we have your support. It won't take long. Just give us 30 focused minutes to talk to you. You'll get more sex if you do this, because when you listen we feel close to you . . . and then we want you!

4) Remember the important dates. Guys, really, whatever it takes. Hey, you don't have a Palm Pilot for nothing! Don't forget the birthday, the anniversary, or any date we've earmarked as significant. You don't have to always remember with a gift . . . just a card, even a kiss works. Big hint . . . if we point the date out to you, it's significant to us. Note it and acknowledge it, even if you have to have it tattooed on your body to do so! Milestone dates that might win you special points if you remember typically include the first date, the first time you said, "I love you," and the day you proposed.

5) Don't lie to us. Guys, why do you lie when you know how much we hate it? I understand you feel the need to lie when you've done something you know we are not going to like, and you'd just rather not deal with our reaction. But I promise, no matter how bad the truth is, if we find out you lied, it's gonna be ten times worse! And we are going to find out some day. Because if it was a small issue, you will forget to cover your own tracks in the future, and boom you will be busted! And if it was a big deal, it usually will have some consequences beyond your control that will come back to haunt you. So just tell us the truth. We'll respect you for being honest even if we are upset with the news. And you never know, if you give us the chance, our reaction may actually surprise you. And don't give us the "technical truth". You know what I mean, the times you respond by avoiding the answer to the question. I call this "guy talk 101". And don't do it!

So as we move on to the next lesson, here are the key things to remember from Lesson #1. No one thinks, behaves, or communicates just like you. Men and women are very different. Our focus, our key drivers, and the way we process information are different. Men are typically results-oriented, driven by accomplishment, and are rational, analytical creatures. Women are typically process-oriented, driven by relationships, and are intuitive, emotional beings. Either gender may possess any of these characteristics in varying degrees. The trick is to figure out where you each fall on the big three. It takes effort to really understand yourself and what things are important to you in life and in a relationship. And it will also take some work to really understand your partner so you can identify where your personal differences lie. These things can work for us, or they can work against us. Our potential for success is dependent on choosing someone who believes in the same big picture of life, then establishing a relationship process that works. And remember, this isn't a magic list. I'm just sharing these thoughts to give you a fresh perspective to consider. I'll bet you had no idea this book was going to give you so much mental exercise!

Chapter 3

Lesson Number Two

"I **AM** a High Maintenance Woman . . . and That's OK!"

Lesson #2 has been much harder to for me to swallow because it is just so personal. Most of my life, guys have been telling me that I am "high maintenance". An intriguing term perhaps, but I did not really understand its meaning. I've asked repeatedly, but over time have found that when put on the spot, no male human I know has been able to verbalize a definition of this secret code name. Of course, it is like any other male code name . . . men know exactly what is means without ever requiring an actual definition. And it is strictly guy code for a woman. Women rarely use high maintenance to define other women. Men would never describe other men in this way. And women don't commonly use the phrase to describe men.

When The Exec and I were separated, I sought to really understand what about myself would cause my high maintenance classification. After all, if I weren't high maintenance would he have left? My search helped me discover that a great part of this term is simply a result of lesson #1, men and women are different.

And when guys feel the impact of those differences, it's a high maintenance moment. The more of those moments, the more high maintenance we are. So now you can see why I say that high maintenance is not necessarily a bad thing. Sometimes it is just guy talk for, "Hey, I really don't get what's going on here, I am uncomfortable." We can safely assume that must be happening a lot based on the fact that we are such different creatures! But sometimes, being called high maintenance is honestly a sign that we need to take a hard look at WHY we are doing what we are doing. Perhaps it's one of those moments when we can't "just let it go"! Maybe it's even an indicator that we have a good opportunity for some personal growth and change!

Ladies, I know what all of you are thinking. "High maintenance women are just bitchy, have an attitude, and spend too much money. They are difficult people, and that's not me." So let's just tackle this misconception right off the bat. I am not telling you that you are difficult. Hey, I would certainly not describe myself as bitchy. I am just telling you something is causing discomfort for your guy. Ok, here's another example. Now we recognize that men hate to be wrong because they are driven by accomplishment, right? And I've shared that I am a person with my own life perspective and some strong opinions. As you can imagine, this frequently puts me in a situation where I am "of a different opinion" than my man. So unless I handle this situation just right, I will make him feel "wrong", like I am not on his side. And so I am thrown into the category of high maintenance for many men. Some guys just don't want to be with a woman who has her own unique ideas. I am not the kind of girl who just goes, "Oh honey, I could just hang on your words all day." Nope, I always have a thought or opinion to add to the conversation. There is nothing wrong with my being a very independent woman. In fact, I would describe it as one of my core strengths. But if I stay conscious of the fact that it makes guys uncomfortable to feel verbally challenged, I can communicate in a way that let's me acknowledge their perspectives while still having my own. In fact, when I look back at conversations I had with The Exec, any time I had a different opinion I would start my sentence, "Well *I* think____!" That would send him the message, "I think you are wrong." Of course, he would immediately go on the defensive with this kind of approach. Now I know I should first say something to acknowledge that I have heard my guy, like, "Yes, I see what you mean, that's very interesting. What do you think about____?" I am able to have my own opinion without putting a guy on the defensive. And this works! Yes, it is a pain in the neck to be this conscious of my communications. But I must use this tactic in my office every day because I work for and with many men with big egos. I still frequently forget to use it, but I'm getting lots better!

So, I've really looked at myself, and I recognize five basic reasons many guys will think I am high maintenance. I think sometimes these just emphasize the differences between men and women, and sometimes they are things I really need to work on! Here's "my short list" of high maintenance characteristics.

1) my savage independence
2) my attention to detail
3) my passion
4) my need for control
5) my impatience

My list starts with the one that always causes problems for me with guys, both in personal and professional relationships. That savage independence thing. Many guys are very intimidated by me . . . after all, I'm someone who doesn't "need" a guy. I make my own money, in fact more than many guys my age. I am quite financially stable. I have my own house. Why wait for a guy to buy a nice place to live and appreciate a tax advantage? I'm a flashy Dallas girl with an exterior "package" that occasionally draws a glance or two. My unique style is a combination of power and spunk. I have actually been completely surprised by many guy friends who tell me that just my "look" can be very scary to men.

Go figure. My level of confidence helps me to speak with authority whenever I open my mouth. I have strong influence and can literally change the direction of a business meeting with one statement. Let's face it. This combination can make me pretty intimidating to a lot of people, but to many men in particular. Remember their need to be "the accomplisher"?

I guess I am very different than what men expect when they see me. My package doesn't scream "brainiac", a stereotype I have to deal with every day. My petite size doesn't really scream aggressive, but that term is probably an accurate description. I think most people are just unprepared for what I really am. Honestly, I haven't quite mastered how to keep these things "in perspective" for people I meet like I am able to do for myself. My parents gave me quite a gift by teaching me to stay grounded, to be appreciative of the gifts I have in life, but to remember it could all be gone tomorrow so not to let it "go to my head". Most people have to really get to know me before they figure out I am not a conceited, bitchy, brat. And in this world, so many people judge you by your look, without even having a conversation. But I recognize that I must manage through my "packaging issue" if I am going to have great relationships because I can honestly intimidate a guy in every way that counts. I guess my challenge is to make a guy feel like "more" instead of "less" with me at his side. I need a man who wants a true partner, not a guy who thinks he should have total control. I could never be with someone who felt he had to make all MY life choices. I waited a long time to grow up and be able to make my own decisions! But despite my independence, I do still want to feel like I'm being "taken care of" in some ways. I'm looking for a partner who will give me emotional support, advice when I need it, and a hug when I've had a bad day. Does that even exist? I am beginning to think it might not.

Number two for me is the attention to detail I have with everything I do. Call me a perfectionist. It is a borderline "need to work on" characteristic, but it really isn't out of control. It is the driver behind why I need to take my time when I get ready. I like to look my best when I go out. Guys, why do you like a pretty girl but hate to wait for her to get fixed up? To this day I cannot do my "reconstruction process" in less than one hour. My attention to detail is also the driver behind my workaholic nature. I cannot do a project at less than 155%. This characteristic will try any guy's patience. I spend lots of money on clothes and how I look. I'm into quality of everything, so it's a good thing I make my own money! I enjoy a great restaurant. I like to sit up front when I go to a concert. I like my house really clean. (Thanks to the The Exec for helping me find the neat freak inside so I could avoid putting "chronic slob" on this list!) This trait can be the driver behind a guy calling me high maintenance because I'm not "wash n' wear", because I'm expensive, because I have high expectations. And to complicate things even more, I want to be with someone who not only can deal with it, but who appreciates my attention to detail. How I look is very important to me, I guess you could say it's my vanity factor. I like to get decked out and to be with someone who notices. But I don't need the attention of the entire room, just my guy. My obsession with great shoes is second only to my addiction to Dr. Pepper. (One of the most intriguing things about Casper is his ability to appreciate my exquisite shoes! Amazing!) Fast food is not a turn off for me. I do enjoy a hop through Burger King. But I want a good balance of great food at great restaurants with my junk food. I love to go out to dinner. And on the job, I cannot stop work on a project until I have pushed myself to what I consider my best work. Always my own worst critic, it is imperative that I feel challenged. And I will go to great lengths to do my best work, whatever it takes. Accomplishing my own lofty goals is part of what keeps me motivated. Will I actually find a guy who can tolerate this one? Do I really think this isn't a great self improvement target? Hmmmmmm.

The third character trait that can nail me as high maintenance is my passion. My emotions are always at maximum. I am passionate about my beliefs, about my work, about love. Everything I do gets my complete commitment and a high level of energy. I am always at mach one with my hair on fire. This means I can be like a roller coaster. When I am happy, which fortunately is most of the time, I am full of life and energy. When I am upset, I cry uncontrollably, but it takes a lot to push me over this edge. When I am mad, you don't want to be hit by my words because they inflict a lot of pain. And because I'm a blend of analytical process with emotional punch, I'm especially dangerous in an argument because I argue with great passion supported by strong logic! I will fight to the death for something in which I believe. Like many women, I am very emotionally resilient and can go from one extreme to the other very quickly. I can be completely exhausting! A guy who has no emotions will never be able to live with me. And guys who have a great deal of emotional depth are rare. I think it is in conflict with their analytical nature. I can honestly say I've only met a few people in my life with a similar mix of emotion and logic.

I'm rarely "on the fence" with anything and am frustrated by those who cannot make decisions. Think things through, make a decision, then commit enough energy to do what you've decided! I cannot grasp why this process is so difficult for so many people. Honestly, there is just as much to lose by not making a decision as by making the wrong one! How can you worry about making a decision due to its potential consequences, but fail to see the consequences of avoiding the decision? How do people go through life just thinking about what they want instead of doing it? I cannot even comprehend wanting something and not just going for it. I am continuously amazed by the fact that most people seem to avoid the tough situations rather than just handling them, but many of my closest friends deal with things this way. Difficult situations usually don't simply disappear because you avoid them . . . they often get much worse!

To complicate this passion of mine, I have tremendous "bandwidth". Call it endless capacity! In fact, I actually need a lot of different responsibilities on my plate to be at my best. This makes me very challenging, because if I have enough energy to perform to the max at work and still manage to give my guy all the attention he needs and then some, I am unforgiving when he can't give back. This level of drive is exhausting for most people I know. If only I had a dollar for every time someone said to me, "If you don't slow down you are going to burn out!" People I work with frequently refer to me as Wonder Woman. I'm a very vivacious person. Will I ever find someone who will actually enjoy this pace and encourage me to chase every dream?

Number four on my list, and my first major "self improvement project", is my need for control. I have faced the fact that I am simply a "control maniac". This is something I never recognized about myself until The Exec told me he wanted a divorce, and this was one of his core reasons. I guess I should remember that part of this is positive. It makes me a very strong leader. I am never intimidated. I will step right in and take over a situation if needed. The Exec told me many times how I was always my strongest in a crisis. But what it delivers on the upside is matched by the downside. I don't listen as well as I should. Sometimes I listen but I don't HEAR because I am too far ahead in my own plan. I have worked very hard to change this. I have become a much better listener in a social setting, but it is still very difficult for me in business. It is almost impossible for me to have an opinion on a topic and not share it. In fact, my driver at work isn't my salary. It is being given projects that give me the opportunity to make a big impact.

In my personal life, this control freak factor can really cause problems. I can never "just accept" anything. I have to discuss it. I must understand it. I am ALWAYS over-analyzing everything. I've really been working on this issue! I don't really think I try to control people on purpose. But sometimes I gain control because I have strong influence. At any rate, when I recognized my major need for control, I was able to see that I was a very judgmental person. Being judgmental would actually be on my list separately if I had not already done so much work to cure myself. It's funny . . . I used to just believe my way was always the right way. It seemed so "matter of fact" to me to consider my opinion the right one. But now, I work hard to remember that you never know what is going on in someone's life that could be driving their behavior, so you cannot judge others. Everyone has their own process, there is no right or wrong approach to life. Part of the fun of being an adult is making your own choices, and we should be able to make choices and do things in a way that feels right to each of us. I am thankful that through my own life experiences I have sometimes reacted in ways I would have formerly judged as negative . . . so now I recognize I have to live by my own rules and respect that others have their own rules. I have worked to accept the fact that what is right and wrong for me might not be the same as what is right and wrong for you.

My control mania was certainly the driver behind my behavior when The Exec told me he wanted a divorce. It was the reason I spent a year trying to change his mind instead of just saying "your loss" and walking away. I'm working on this. I think I have made a little progress, and Casper would be the one to tell me if it was successful. Anytime we discussed his relationship situations, I tried to remember to do more listening than talking, and to be sure to remind him that he needed to make his own decisions based on what was "right" for him. At times I kept my opinions completely to myself because it was so important for me to know that I had not influenced his life choices. This control mania is probably my worst habit, and I know it's a big one. I'm trying to balance in favor of the positive side, focusing only on a little influence instead of total control. (Completely losing this would be "unBeth"!) Things that impact me that are beyond my control are very hard for me to deal with. I have not yet mastered releasing myself from responsibility for things beyond my control. It causes me great stress when I have to deal with things beyond my control. I drive myself nuts trying to think of some thing I can do, some action I can take. Recognizing that I cannot fix everything and cannot make it all better . . . it's just almost an impossible thought for me. I hope that God will give me the strength some day to master it. In the meantime, I'm just trying to learn to just let some things go . . . but it's hard!

Finally my lack of patience comes into play. I'm not always impatient, only when I really want something. In fact, there are many times when I've found an endless supply of patience. But when I set a goal, I just go for it full force. You will never find me sitting back and waiting for anything. I have a core belief that God may present us with opportunities, but it is our choice to go for them or not. I never want to have to say, "I wish I had just tried____." Frequently I cause my own internal struggles simply because I cannot wait. I find that I am very easily frustrated. I would never be able to do business in Asia since they are so patient in their negotiations! I need to go close the deal NOW! When I fall in love, I go hard and fast. Sometimes I don't give things time to really develop in a relationship. Actually, all of my four big relationships were like that. I fell hard and fast and didn't really get to know any of those guys like I should have before I was completely invested in the deal. In fact, I might not have married hubby #1, Mr. Porsche, if I had not been so impatient. And I probably wouldn't have ended the relationship with My Cowboy if I weren't so impatient. (Although isn't seven years patient????) My impatience makes me high maintenance for myself just as much as for anyone else. But I recognize it will benefit me to learn to allow things to unfold at their own pace and in their own way more frequently than I do. Perhaps this is also fueled by my need for control. I have to be driving whatever is happening. If nothing else, this last ordeal with Casper has forced me to work on my patience!

So how did I become this high maintenance creature? What did I go through in life that gave me this unique combination of five factors that will make me a challenge for most of the men on the planet? Can I stay myself and have a successful permanent relationship? At this point I'm not really sure there is a man out there who will be able to accept all my little "qualities", and for me that is a very scary thought. Looking back through my life has helped me understand how I grew up to be who I am. It has been the first step in understanding what is important for me in life and what aspects about myself are things I want to change. This self-review has given me a clear perspective for going forward.

My parents were certainly the driving force behind my savage independence. My mom was "in charge". She made a lot of the decisions and is still the pillar of strength in my family. It is funny how much I am like my mother. She is the one who made me strong enough to ask questions when I don't believe in a decision. My father gave me the confidence to have no fear. He still tells me every time we talk, "You can do it," with any project I undertake. I guess most parents try to give their children confidence and independence. My parents accomplished it. My sisters also played a big role in my development. I am a little like each of them in a few respects. My passion for life was certainly in part a gift from my sister Bindy, who always displayed an endless supply of energy. We both are very emotional like my father. My sister Barbara was my example that I could be whatever I wanted . . . she was simultaneously the valedictorian of her class and a "Kawasaki Cutie". She always approached things her way and lives her life by her own rules to this day. I hope that I am even a quarter as kind as my oldest sister B. J. She and my father both played a major role in developing my ability to forgive just about anything. She is extremely even-keeled, almost never raises her voice . . . ahhh, it would benefit me to pick up that one! My drive and independence are outgrowths of the strength my family gave to me.

And I have to look at all this and be realistic for my own future relationships. I need to be with a man who has a great deal of confidence, and who is not intimidated by my independence. I have to recognize this is the core of my personality, and it is not going anywhere. While I know I want to make some adjustments in my behavior, my sense of who I am is positive. I think that behaviors are things that can be changed, but I believe the core of yourself is your constant and the foundation for your life. And it is critically important to understand the core of your personality before you can find someone who will complement it.

My "flash factor" comes from many places. Part of it comes from growing up in Dallas, where women are always looking their best. I know many people think Dallas is a very "plastic" town, a place where how you look is more important than anything else. But I lived there over twenty-five years of my life and strongly disagree with the city's superficial reputation. The people in Texas are among the most genuine and friendly I have ever met. Having said that, I do recognize that my attention to my appearance was heavily influenced by my environment. On a stage dancing and in pageants by age five, I became very comfortable having my hair done and wearing makeup very early in life. In fact, my mom frequently used to curl my hair for school. I loved it. My mother has always been a very beautiful woman. I can remember looking at photos of her when I was growing up and hoping I would look like her some day. She taught me to enjoy a great sense of style and designed some amazing clothes for me. For as long as I can remember, clothes were very important to me. My sister Bindy also had a great sense of style and had a big influence on me in this respect. She taught me how to "shop till ya drop", a gift for which I will forever be grateful!

And then we have the cheerleader experience. As a Dallas Cowboys Cheerleader, I can say I was exposed to the "high maintenance training capital of the world". Thirty-six of the most beautiful girls in Dallas, encouraged to be certain to look their best at all times. We were never without makeup, not even at practice for hours in the heat of Texas Stadium as we never knew when photographers would be present. We always had to have our nails done so our hands would look nice while signing autographs. I think that "big hair" was invented by the Cowboy Cheerleaders. In fact, if you drive by the stadium the weekend of auditions, be careful not to light a match or the place might explode from all the hair spray! This is actually the REAL reason for the hole in the top of Texas Stadium! But despite the emphasis on how we looked, this group was also fundamental in my development in so many important ways. The majority of the girls with whom I cheered were extremely nice... I know you would prefer to believe them brainless bimbettes, but you would be wrong. I learned so much about performing from this group... that it takes more than a smile to win a crowd, it takes charisma. I have the Dallas Cowboys Cheerleaders to thank for giving me the ability to use my charisma as a skill, to consciously use it when I deliver business presentations to connect with my audience. The group gave me opportunities to interface with strangers all the time, and I became capable of handling myself in large group meetings and events with ease. My company has relocated me five times and I have been able to easily meet new people both in my new offices and new cities. I have always had an outgoing personality. I think the team just helped enhance it. The DCC certainly contributed to the confidence my parents helped develop. I think the DCC also gave me a "trooper" attitude, to handle everything with a smile. When I recently went back for a reunion, we were all out on the field to rehearse the halftime honorary ceremony. It was raining and just 40 degrees. Yet most of the hundred women on that field were laughing and having a good time anyway, despite being soaking wet and freezing cold. So I know when I look for a partner now, I need someone who also has that trooper attitude, who can deal with the fact that I will always need some primp time, and who isn't going to get jealous from my flirty personality. One of my favorite things about Casper is that his positive attitude comes out through his ability to handle adverse situations very lightly. I think this is a very rare ability and one of the things I have always believed could make us good potential partners... we both like life "light."

I don't think you can add value in a relationship unless you are comfortable with yourself. My sense of who I am is very strong. I know the kinds of things I want to achieve in life. I know the kind of relationships I want to have, and my order of priorities is very clear. I highly recommend you take a look at yourself very closely. Get to know yourself! Spend some time really understanding what is important for you. Look openly at your strengths as well as your weaknesses. Don't be afraid to admit your imperfections. After all, everyone has them. Heck, people pay hundreds of dollars a month in therapy to go through this process. Why not treat yourself to the benefits for free? Write these things down. Make a list of things that you consider key for your life. Make notes of the things you want to change, and give yourself some baby steps to make those changes happen. Recognize your positive qualities. Learn to consciously rely on your strengths and enhance them.

My relationship failures have certainly given me a lot of pain to deal with, but the benefit has been that I understand what I need for success the next time. And that is priceless! I know that I am a lot like the character Scarlett O'Hara, and I am looking for Rhett Butler. (Have you seen "Gone with the Wind"? If not, please consider it required viewing in your near future!) Scarlett was fiercely independent, extremely vivacious, very determined, and completely her own woman. Rhett was a man who was fiercely independent himself, a bit of a rebel, confident, living life by his rules, and a tall, dark, and handsome scoundrel to boot! I recognize I need someone who can balance me out, and that is going to take a very strong man. I may be looking for my own Rhett Butler for a very long time. Today I am not at all convinced the Rhett Butler type actually exists . . . but Casper comes dangerously close! However, I recognize it will be better to be alone and comfortable with life by myself for a while than to be in an unhappy relationship. Being all alone is very difficult for me because having a solid relationship is the most important thing for me in life. A great relationship is central to my happiness, and I'm off balance without someone special to share the great things in life.

So, from this chapter, the important take away for you is that an understanding of yourself is the beginning to having the ability to build a strong relationship. You must be honest with yourself about what is important to you and what your priorities are. I have just taken you though the tiniest bit of my own self-exploration. I have admitted to you and to myself that I AM high maintenance. And high maintenance is not a bad thing. It's just an indication that someone does not know where you are coming from. It is absolutely ok to have imperfections. Just recognize what they are and how they impact your behavior. Know yourself, be yourself, and find someone who will be in sync with you on life issues. People, life is just way too short trying to spend it attempting to get on the same page with your partner. Start on the same page, and you will find life so much easier!

Chapter 4

Lesson Number Three

"Live in the Reality, **NOT** the Fantasy"

Of all lessons I have learned, and those I will inevitably learn in the future, one of the hardest for me so far has been Lesson #3. It's clear . . . I have a bad, bad habit. I get caught up in the fantasy of how I want things to be, and then I stay there, no matter what unfolds before my very eyes. Isn't it funny how it is entirely possible to hear only what you want to hear, to completely ignore the reality of the situation, and just see what you want to see? Honestly, you can see just about anything if you look hard enough. Looking back on all four of my relationship crashes, I can honestly say I have done this every single time. You would think I might have recognized this problem before now. But no, it takes me thirteen years, a broken first love, two failed marriages, and a painful affair to see this one clearly. And the really sad part is that I keep getting progressively worse instead of better! People, please don't learn this lesson the hard way like I have!

Let's look at my last two failures for some good examples of how NOT to handle your life situations. You have already been lightly introduced to the harsh departure of my second husband, The Exec. Ok, let me share a little more detail. We'd had one tough year on top of what I considered five great ones. I'd left my cushy corporate job in September of 1995 to shoot two fitness videos and start a small video company. I was going to be the CEO and he was going to be the COO. We would run the company together when it became hugely successful. It was certainly a heavenly fantasy. But when I didn't have huge sales right from the first advertisement, and overnight success was obviously not going to happen, things began to get very difficult. The Exec was very resentful that I was losing money invested by friends and business associates, as well as cash of our own. I was frustrated that at the first sign things weren't just going to be an exploding overnight success, he expected me to truly just throw in the towel and say, "Gee, sorry everyone, this wasn't as easy as I thought, so I'm done." I am not a quitter, and I thought my intense dedication was one of the reasons he'd been attracted to me in the first place. Needless to say, there was a great deal of tension for several months. Rather than addressing it, we just did not discuss the situation so that we could avoid arguing. So unfortunately, our frustration with each other just grew and grew. But nothing we were dealing with was impacting my feelings for him, and I couldn't imagine that something as stupid as money could impact his feelings for me. And I was so wrong.

We transferred with our company back to Texas from Chicago in July of 1996, as I was returning to my corporate career there. He had chosen to take a position in Ft. Worth rather than an overseas assignment because I did not really want to live in Asia at that time. My father had undergone a quadruple bypass just months before. The Exec's father had recently passed away from the same type of heart problems, and I was honestly feeling a need to be close to my family. He made the job choice for me so I could be close to my family, but then he held me responsible for his decision and was very resentful. He did not like his big change in lifestyle with his new position. He was too accustomed to flying in first class all over the world, negotiating with senior government officials, and spending time with "the Prince at the palace" building the necessary relationships to close major business deals. Having a normal executive role at a giant corporation dealing with U.S. company presidents wasn't fulfilling for him any more. Since The Exec was never satisfied with anything, this should not have surprised me. He saw me as "the cause" of this new bad life he had acquired. But he didn't bother to tell me. He just allowed our transfer to progress forward, taking me to look at houses and planning our future. All this while telling our realtor in confidence that he was going to divorce me and giving her his own criteria for housing since he was planning to handle it on his own income. One night when I came home from a trip and could tell he was frustrated, I made the mistake of asking what was wrong. His response was four words that haunted me for the next year . . ."I want a divorce." I spent hours trying to get him to explain what was wrong. We hadn't had a less than perfect relationship for very long. Certainly we were enough in love that we could fix anything we chose to fix. Again, I was wrong. In fact, his decision was made, and he did not want to discuss anything but "the plan" for how to draft the ending of our marriage.

He explained that he had made choices in his life, because of me, that he believed were compromises. He decided that I caused him to make "bad" decisions, even when the choices were his own. He felt he shouldn't have to compromise, that he should have whatever he wanted. I had too much influence, and no matter how hard he tried, he just couldn't eliminate me from his mental decision process. DUH. When you love someone, you can't help but consider that person in your decision process. That's normal. When you share a life with someone, you will have some compromises. It isn't normal to just go through life getting whatever you want whenever you want it. To expect the world to constantly rotate around you is a selfish perspective. Life just isn't that easy. Looking back, I think maybe it didn't feel "normal" for The Exec to care about someone else more than himself. I think it just felt wrong to him to consider giving up things he felt were important. He was just too accustomed to living on "Planet Me". He felt I had too much control and he hated compromise. He gave me an ultimatum that I had to agree to a divorce if I wanted to prove that I really loved him and give us any chance for a future. At this point, I should have said, "Selfish bastard, I am thrilled that you are out of my life!" But instead, I thought, "Oh this poor frustrated man who loves me so much it completely confuses him." Can you believe that? I thought he was having a midlife crisis and he would work his way through it. No matter what, I believed his love for me would conquer all. NOT the case . . . see lesson #7!

We found out that Texas has a state law that requires you to be a resident of the state for six months before you can file for divorce. I saw this as a "sign" that the divorce was a big mistake and tried to convince him it was divine intervention. Have you ever felt you were having divine intervention? I can clearly remember many life moments when it seemed that God intervened on my behalf right before my eyes, and I simply thought this was another. He disagreed, and his solution was to have me check with Illinois and determine if we could file there instead. We couldn't. So for six months I attempted to convince him the divorce was a mistake. I took him on a fabulous trip to Las Vegas for Christmas. I went into my research process and tried to identify any way I could change myself to make him want me. I wrote him letter after letter to try and show him I was learning to do things differently. Most importantly, I was actually willing to do anything differently if he would just give us a chance. I would have become a completely different person if I had thought it would work. Don't EVER do that, because you cannot be successful in a long term relationship if you are presenting an imaginary version of yourself. I was so desperate for his love, I was totally blind to the reality. I was stuck in that fantasy that love would triumph!

Well, to keep me from taking him to the cleaners financially, he caved in to some degree, and we did spend a few months dating on and off. And of course, he wasn't just dating me, he was also seeing other women. The entire time, he never stopped the divorce progress. He insisted that if I wanted any chance for a future I had to allow this "paperwork" to happen so it could be out of "the way" of any chance we might have. It was a very manipulative move, and I allowed myself to be taken advantage of because I was so focused on showing him I was capable of giving up control. My friends were all ready to throw me off a cliff to help me see what was really happening. Despite multiple attempts by all of my friends to convince me he wasn't really going to reconcile with me, I couldn't see it. I just dealt with the pain of him dating other women, filing divorce paperwork, and leaving me with all the debt from the failure of our business. It was horrible. And I have to take all the blame for my pain because I gave it to myself. I refused to look at the reality of my situation. That love wasn't going to conquer all. That my husband, whom I loved so deeply, was absolutely capable of walking away from me without trying to fix whatever was wrong with our marriage. That he cared more about keeping himself financially protected than about any potential our relationship had.

But I finally saw it, and yes, it took a harsh encounter to knock sense into my head. It was August of 1997, about a year after he first told me he wanted a divorce, and it had been final for about a month. We were both transferring away from Texas. He was going to China, I was headed to Florida. I had offered to go with him to China. He said ok and actually allowed me to ask the company to move me there. But my best career opportunity was in Florida, and when I told him about it, he explained he was completely relieved because he really didn't want me to go to China anyway. He was going to let me move to China rather than to be honest with me! The night before I moved, I went to his house to say goodbye, and he was there with another girl. He came to the door with lipstick on his face. When I asked him who she was he simply said, "Someone who will miss me when I move." I was furious!!! So I parked up the street and called his house every 15 minutes until she left. Then I broke down and called him later from my hotel and asked him to come over and talk. When he arrived, he explained to me for the hundredth time that he was disappointed in our marriage because he thought we would have more money, more power, more status, etc. I finally started to get it. I said, "You don't marry someone because you think they will improve your social standing or your bank account. You marry them because their smile makes you feel like a million dollars." He said my smile hadn't done a thing for him in a really long time. And then I finally saw that he wasn't in love with me anymore at all. And that was the moment I began the slow process of recovery, the moment I let go of the fantasy that some day we would be back together. And it was the moment I faced the harsh reality that I was only thirty-two, already divorced for the second time, and very much alone. I felt so defective, like I was "less" because I had been divorced TWICE. Sometimes I still feel that way, and I hate it. It's like I'm just a complete relationship failure. I'm not sure if he ever was honestly in love with me. I don't know if he is even capable of honest love. But at least now I can look back and see the reality I was unable to deal with at the time. I just lived in my "love will conquer all" fantasy, thinking that despite everything that happened he was going to come running back to me. Ha. And I swore I would never allow myself to be hurt like that again.

Yeah, right. So I moved right back into fantasyland with Casper. It was only a month and a half after I moved to Florida that we met, October of 1997. Although I had been living by myself for over a year, I had been so focused on trying to save my marriage that I never considered seeing anyone else. And so I experienced my third period of horrible loneliness. Truly, my recovery from The Exec had just begun. My initial fall for Casper was as much about the fantasy of a new chance at love as it was about him. After all, he is about as close to Rhett Butler in the flesh as you can get, minus the slick southern accent. Casper is about as deadly as a man can be. He is incredibly handsome, such a "manly man", very distinguished looking, chivalrous to the end. He is extremely smart with quite a quick wit. He makes me laugh easily. When we have a conversation, it's like the entire room is completely filled with our energy. I can say with complete conviction that I believe Casper to be the most intelligent man I've ever met. He is very responsible, well established, and romantic to the core, with just a hint of totally obvious bad boy in there somewhere. IRRESISTABLE!

At first, it was such a harmless flirt over e-mail. That lasted for about two months. He took me to his house one day to see his construction progress, and that was the day he kissed me for the first time. We'd had this little banter over e-mail back and forth about needing some mistletoe because Christmas was approaching, and on the way up to his house he asked me if I had any with me. I actually lost my balance and almost fell when he kissed me. I never got past my sense of "nervous teenager" with him. From that point, he was telling me that Snow White was moving in with her mother when he was ready to move into his house. I felt so bad for him, going through such a major breakup during the holidays. He let me believe that she was moving in with her mom until the night before they moved into the house together. And that night I got this mysterious little message from him on my pager, telling me he was so sorry, but he could not end his relationship with Snow White.

For the next eight months, we were all over the board with our communications. We had periods when we didn't really talk mixed with many steamy e-mail conversations. Snow White actually moved out of the house for a week in March of 1998, and we spent some amazing time together, starting with an incredible all night conversation at his place the first night she was gone, and ending with one sultry "near miss" night in my hot tub! We shared many meals and spent a lot of time talking over coffee. It was every bit as romantic as it sounds, but as I look back I think we were honestly just beginning a friendship. I did make an attempt to do a little dating. I had exactly three dates with three guys after Casper and Snow White reconciled, but was quickly convinced I'd rather be by myself than play the dating game. I think the fantasy of being in a relationship with Casper was enough because I was still recovering from the pain of losing my marriage. It didn't matter that we weren't actually dating. There was no rush. The fantasy of a relationship with the man of my dreams was enough, for a while.

And then the travel happened. In August of 1998, Casper and I both ended up out of town at the same time on business. And that was the first of many nights of sex that changed my life. In fact, I hadn't really known what I had been missing! And it was also the groundwork for a true and deep friendship, and the point at which I honestly began to fall, hard! Believe me, I only thought I was in deep before the travel time. We both traveled to the same city every week for the next two months. We took the same flights, sometimes we rode in the limo together to the airport. We went to dinner, to some great clubs, and played in the snow. Our personalities have always mixed like nothing I've ever experienced. Our mental chemistry was completely intoxicating for me. Spending any time with Casper felt amazing, totally natural, very uplifting. When we began traveling together, I felt vibrant and alive for the first time in months. I was convinced he was my prince and that my little Cinderella story was going to come true. I had my fantasy life out of town Monday through Thursday and slipped back to my reality life over the weekends. It was very difficult to deal with, but I was trying so hard to believe in our future. And then the holidays came and messed with us. Can you imagine how it feels to have to deal with the man you are falling in love with celebrating Christmas with the person he swears he is leaving? I wanted to storm his house and demolish his decorations! Not to mention the fact that I felt extremely sorry for myself, enduring my third set of holidays in a row as a single girl. It was a miserable and difficult time.

And then the unthinkable – he came back from his Christmas vacation engaged. I was ready to die! I felt used. I felt stupid. But mostly, I felt hurt to my core. How could he have been so close to this with her and have been telling me he was leaving her? It was so hard to understand. We talked about it for a long time one afternoon, and he explained that he had been seeing a counselor who convinced him his relationship problem was his own fear of commitment. He told me that he had to take that step, to know whether or not it was true. I was skeptical, but I wanted to believe in my dream, even if that meant I had to ignore the reality. And then the travel started again in January of 1999. He asked for the chance to talk, and of course, I wanted to talk. After all, as Cinderella, I was entitled to have a happy ending someday. He assured me he was certain the engagement was an important mistake. Important because it helped him know it wasn't the right step. Of course I believed him. And things became just like they were before his engagement, in fact maybe even a little bit better. Great conversation, great times, great sex, I thought certainly he was ready to end things with her. It honestly seemed he was going to try. I accepted that job transfer referenced earlier to Chicago and was very nervous that our relationship would begin to decline when I moved, but it did not seem to hinder our progress at first. He convinced me he would also consider a transfer. It was actually a relief not having to see him around town with Snow White.

The big opportunity for Casper to take action came when he had a business trip to Europe in April of 1999. He made a passing comment that he wished I could go, so I jumped on it and offered to join him. He was planning to end his engagement before he left. He felt that he was going to have a better chance of ending his relationship if he was removed from Snow White a little bit. Heading off to a foreign country would be helpful. We both agreed that unless he went through with it, I would not join him. He did, so a few days later I hopped a plane and we spent five incredible days in Europe. On the way back, we visited his brother's restaurant and he introduced me to some of his family. He told his brother Snow White had moved out and that I would be joining him for their millenium party the upcoming New Year's Eve. His brother seemed very supportive, telling him he always felt his relationship with Snow White was more father/daughter than the kind of partnership you have to have to make a marriage work. I remember the exact moment we parted at the airport, each heading to our new separate cities. I felt like we were being ripped apart. It was as though we would never see each other again.

And indeed it was the last time we spent more than five minutes together until November 1999, seven months later. Things rapidly deteriorated after the Europe trip. He couldn't talk to me. He said he just felt so guilty. He told me Snow White was devastated by their broken engagement and he was just trying to be as tender as possible. And then they reconciled, and he began to just ignore me, so I did the unthinkable. I contacted Snow White and told her about our relationship. It was very difficult for me to do, but I honestly felt like he really wanted to be with her, and I had done her a horrible injustice. I needed to tell her I was sorry so I could clear the path for him to be honest with her and repair their relationship. I apologized and told her there was no excuse for my behavior. Then I told her to be careful, because I was not the first time he had been unfaithful. He told me some things in Europe about others in his past. The minute I did it, I had instant regret. I was just trying to absolve myself from the guilt. If I'd just been able to deal with it on my own, I could have spared Snow White so much pain. Of course, Casper and I stopped communicating for a while, but then I made contact because I just couldn't stand it. And of course, he told me how he missed me and that he wished he had handled things differently. But what Casper didn't tell me was that Snow White was not really the cause of our abrupt ending. He had begun to see another woman with whom he'd been having an affair on and off for several years. He had actually told me a bit about her our last night in Europe, but classified her as a "pre-existing condition" to our relationship and described her as someone who just refused to let him go. I'll call her "Taz", short for Tasmanian Devil because she is a whirlwind of raw emotion. What a mess! We had a few more months of wireless messages over two-way pagers. It had become our primary method of communication after my transfer. But our communications were hesitant because we did not have the same trust for each other that had made the friendship happen in the first place. In September 1999,

I sent him this really personal, really profound e-mail explaining why I needed to walk away from the relationship, and go figure. Snow White was checking his work e-mail and read it before he did. I created another huge issue for him simply by attempting to make a final graceful exit.

We saw each other twice in November 1999. The first time, he was in Chicago on business. We talked things through a little bit . . . he made a move on me and I resisted. The next day we had coffee and had a good talk and agreed we would attempt to do a little starting over. The second was a one day fling when I was on a business trip back in Florida. But it didn't feel the same for either of us. And of course it wasn't, because everything we had started to build had been stopped . . . so I thought. And then he tells me that he actually thinks he has very strong feelings for Taz, and he thinks he wants to end his engagement and try a real relationship with her. Neat. Reflect with me on the reality I refused to see. He's engaged to Snow White. He thinks he's in love with Taz. He is reasonably sure he doesn't want to be with me. But, instead of saying, "Buh-bye," like we all know I should, I give my fantasy the benefit of the doubt. I knew it would be very hard for him to actually leave Snow White. I was going to believe in his motivations, despite the fact that there was every probability this thing between us was just the manipulation of the century. I told myself it was obvious he loves Snow White like she's his child and feels completely responsible for her. You can love your child and your life partner differently but simultaneously, yes? He seems to have some of the right feelings towards Taz, yet I feared that he was just acting on his sense of "do what's right" because she had been happily married until their affair and was now planning to leave her husband for him. After all, if he was really in love with her, I would never have been in the picture, right? I hear what he's saying and I tell him to be with Taz if that is truly what he wants. But then he tells me part of the issue is that I'm living in Chicago. So I hop a plane to Florida to visit him and ask him to join me out of town for a few days to spend time to remind us both what we had.

Chicago was filled with nothing but stress for me. I was having a horrible time trying to get construction started on a loft downtown, hated the weather, and was isolated from most of my family and friends. So I ask my company to allow me to move back to Florida and do my job that I love in the place I am personally happy. The company says yes, but Casper says no, and I accept that he must truly want to be with Taz.

But the move's been put in motion, so I go back to Florida for four days in December of 1999 to find a house. I am determined to at least get to a friendly place with him that allows us to be comfortable as friends now that we'll be in the same city again. We have coffee and chat. He tells me he misses me, and here we go again. We get a little flirty over pagers, have some coffee, and one night he comes over to my hotel and we have what was absolutely the steamiest sex of the entire relationship to that point. He tells me he must "go wrap up loose ends" and will be back later that night. He doesn't come back, but we then have a week and a half of very intense 'virtual sex' over our two-way pagers. I was getting sucked back in, but recognized that he was very confused and this was definitely back to square one for us at best. And I was completely comfortable with that because I saw a new start happening. I felt the relationship kicking up another notch. Or so I thought . . . I was now going to learn my next hard lesson . . . beware of the M.O.D.!

So what on earth are you supposed to grasp from all this? Keep your eyes wide open and your feet on the floor. Do not get so caught up in your fantasy that you cannot clearly see the reality. Do not get caught up in the words you want to hear, and do not read between the lines because you will inevitably hear words that were not actually spoken! Each relationship has potential, but that doesn't mean the circumstances will be right for you to reach the potential. The Exec was not the right person for me. I can clearly see that now. But there was no convincing me of that at the time. I had to see it for myself. Casper was a heavy dose of bad timing but enough magic that he resurrected the dream I thought I had lost forever. I'm not so naïve that I'd tell you that everything should always be simple and clean, that you should never fall for someone who is already in a relationship. I have been through too many of my own experiences that have helped me learn it isn't that easy or pretty. But don't be afraid to ask yourself hard questions and make yourself give honest answers. My tough question with Casper is, "What the heck am I doing stuck on someone who doesn't see enough in front of him to take action he says he wants to take????" I still can't answer that question. I have to accept these things I cannot control, I have to just let go of that fantasy and live in the reality. I only wish I could have asked myself some really tough questions before I learned the next lesson. Do yourselves a big favor people, don't go through life with blinders on. You will save yourselves years of pain.

Chapter 5

Lesson Number Four

"Beware of the **M.O.D.**!"

Ok, I thought lesson #3 was hard, but this one takes the cake. Ladies, you are going to hate this chapter. Guys, unfortunately you will probably marvel at the story that unfolds. Personally, if I saw this on TV I would say it was impossible and unrealistic. The fact is, my whole relationship with Casper is indeed in the running for "the deception of the century". Guys, you saw this coming didn't you? Casper might just be the ultimate M.O.D. . . . Master of Deception! He is a person blessed with truly amazing qualities, but sometimes he uses those qualities to accomplish the most devious endeavors. Let's get back into the story. Remember I will be moving back to Florida soon. Casper has told me how he misses me, and we've shared a very erotic night together. It's December 1999, we've had steamy virtual pager sex for two weeks. I'm feeling our relationship might finally materialize this time and am looking forward to our fresh start when I get this anonymous message on my pager one Thursday night, "FYI: the wedding is a go. They are going to be married this weekend . . ." My whole fantasy crashes before my eyes in 60 seconds. The pages continue . . . I am told he is using both me and Taz and bragging about it. I'm told that many people know, except the three of us. I am mortified! My reputation is important to me, and having to imagine people knowing about this situation kills me. The anonymous source also tells me Taz is receiving some pages as well. I'm trying to identify the messenger. I actually banter back and forth for almost six hours while I have my paging service provider try to track the source with no luck. I'm disturbed because this person understands many intimate details of my private life. Frankly, I feel a bit violated! But I am grateful, because I recognize it is probably true and I've just been spared the pain of the same type of "Christmas Surprise" I'd been given the year before with the engagement.

So I remain calm, get as much info from this person as I possibly can, and page Casper first thing the next morning. I explain I've been told he is getting married and ask if it is true. He responds two hours later with, "I know that rumor is going around." Now, to a guy, this is not a lie, but to a woman, this is a HUGE lie. Technically, he just avoided the question. (Remember how I told you guys NOT to do this????) I'm mortified when I receive his page, because I recognize "guy talk 101" and I know what it means . . . he's indeed getting married that weekend. But I realize I am going to be able to get past him, because he has gotten married and I'm not falling for anymore of his sweet talk, my pain will be over, and things can get no worse.

And then the unthinkable, it actually DOES get worse. Monday morning, I receive a call from Taz. She thinks I actually sent the pages to her . . . after all, who else could have all this detail. I explain that I received similar pages. We begin to compare. We discover that the entire time he has been telling us BOTH the same kinds of lies. He has presented me to her as this desperate psycho that has to have him and will stop at nothing to get him. He has called me manipulative. It is unbelievable, but I am more hurt by how he presented me to her than by the fact he was seeing Taz at the same time! Of course, remember that he had said similar things about Taz to me . . . that no matter what he said or did she would just not go away. While he was having coffee with me, he was paging Taz telling her I just "showed up" and wanted to talk. He told her I just couldn't grasp that he wanted to be with her. Of course, the coffee visit was something we discussed days in advance. And he's sending her these pages while he's sitting there telling me, "I miss you." He was with her the night we had coffee, while he was paging me to let me know he wanted to come see me at the hotel. The next night after our steamy hotel visit, he called Taz on his way home "just to hear her voice", and he told us both he was ending his relationship with Snow White that night. Remember, this is two weeks prior to his wedding and honeymoon.

Our trip to Europe that I thought was so special was not. Taz had almost gone as well, and he was managing through both of us willing to join him with the ultimate skill and grace. He was covering this with me by saying things like, "I may be so depressed it might not be a good idea for you to come. I want to be sure only the right people from work are there so it won't look bad that I ended the engagement and went right off with you." And I bought every word of it. He told Taz that he went to Europe alone and hung out with a local girl he met. And this is just the tip of the iceberg of lies. The level of betrayal is incomprehensible to me. It was so calculated. It was so devious. It was downright malicious. I am amazed that I could have actually been this stupid. Say it with me, "Love is BLIND!"

The most painful thing to me at this point wasn't that he was with someone else or even that he had gotten married. It surprises me, but the most disturbing thing was that I honestly believed he respected me, if nothing else, as a friend. And here it appeared I wasn't really even his friend. Was I just another notch on a REALLY long list? It made me sick to consider that possibility. Taz and I talked and paged each other for the entire two weeks he was away on his honeymoon. It's borderline twisted to be bonding with a woman with whom he betrayed me. But she understood, had lived the same thing, and knew how I could have been sucked in by the lies. And yes, people, he *IS* that good at it. Taz is funny and smart, and I genuinely like her. Isn't it sad that here he has two beautiful, intelligent, fun women completely in love with him, and who knows how many more, and he chooses to stay with a person who doesn't make him happy? Maybe he had to choose Snow White, someone completely dependent and insecure who allows him to take care of her in every way, simply because it makes him feel great to be so needed. Maybe he needs someone very naïve because any strong intelligent woman would eventually see through him and walk away. Ok, granted, it took a really long time, but I did finally see it! I think the problem for Taz and for me was pretty simple . . . we both believed he wanted to live his life differently, and each of us believed we were the reason behind his desire to change. And I'm sure that was part of the attraction. Of course, there is also the possibility that he's deeply in love with Snow White and just needs a lot of sex on the side. Think about it . . . two nice girls, one unhappy in her marriage, one divorced who could relate to his confused feelings, and neither out there sleeping with anyone else. It's about as safe as you could be in pursuing multiple women!

You'd think the wedding would be enough to end the fantasy for Taz or for me. But no!! I've gone round after round with Casper, and Taz has never left his side. He's always had to convince me that his relationship with Taz was over to pull me back in, and I've always believed it . . . only to find it was untrue. And Snow White . . . well, I've always accepted his "ending is in progress", though I've gotten some interesting stories about that situation as well. Now, keep in mind that Taz and I have several mutual friends and have also maintained some level of personal contact. From time to time, Taz and I would also receive some eye opening alert from that "anonymous pager" who sent the wedding message. Oh, did I fail to mention that Snow White and I also have some mutual friends? Yes indeedy, he was actually able to pull off major relationships with three closely connected women simultaneously!! He's a very talented guy! I look back and realize that the fact that he could convince any of us that the others were out of his life is nothing less than amazing. And we are all just as responsible, we knew better. We just didn't want to accept it because we each believed he was sincerely a great guy. Good people sometimes make very bad choices and hurt the ones they love. We each were so focused on the great things in our relationships, we chose to ignore the bad. His behavior was inexcusable, and I'm not trying to tell you it was ok. I just want you to understand the thoughts that kept us each hanging on.

Casper, Taz, and I have had several major explosions, ignited each time one of us would find out he was still sleeping with the other. All this was happening despite the fact that he was still married to and living with Snow White. It started immediately upon the return from his honeymoon, when he worked hard to convince Taz and me that he was sincere to some level with each of us. He told me he was deeply in love with Taz, that I was his best friend, and that his marriage was a huge mistake. He really seemed torn apart. He told Taz and me that he and Snow White eloped, and that he was not going to turn in his paperwork to make it legal. I actually felt sorry for him. I tried to be supportive and to help him convince Taz he was indeed in love with her. And I was very happy that we were indeed the best of friends.

And then, after a few months, he started to drop little hints that he wanted to be with me, that despite his genuine love for Taz he couldn't imagine being in a long-term relationship with her. He convinced me it was horribly difficult for him to end his relationship with Taz because his feelings were so strong, but that he desperately wanted out. He seemed to genuinely believe their relationship just couldn't work, but he appeared to be completely controlled by his emotions for her. Of course, I only had to look at my own feelings for him and the many times I'd wanted to walk away... only to find I wasn't strong enough... to understand. He did all kinds of things to convince me. He sent her pages telling her he needed to end the relationship and copied me so I'd know he'd done it. He actually sat down with both of us and admitted to Taz in front of me that he had deep feelings for us both . . . and she didn't even listen to the words come out of his mouth. She just heard the things she wanted to hear and refused to believe the rest. That is exactly what we do when we are caught up in the fantasy, remember? We each got so many different stories out of him in private, it was impossible to know the real truth. I watched Taz refuse to let go of their relationship no matter what he did or said . . . and I recognized that I could not allow myself to be in that situation. I saw Taz making the same mistakes I had with The Exec, and I knew she would have to see it herself before things in her life could change. She was deeply in love with him. Casper told me she would try and talk him out of any decision he made to walk away from her. And I believed him, because I could see she was stuck at a place I'd been myself. I understood and felt sorry for her. Remember, I spent a year trying to talk The Exec out of leaving me.

She asked me repeatedly what she could do and was very disturbed when my answer was, "Nothing, he has to make his own choice." And of course, he wasn't helping the matter by raising concerns about their relationship, then madly professing his love for her. It's really hard to process that someone can be in love with you, but not want to be with you. I think he just always wanted to insure that we each believed he had some sincere feelings, because if he couldn't convince us of that . . . this "love quadrangle" was truly the ugliest situation imaginable. At first, Taz and I tried to be friends to some degree. But the reality of the situation was that this "friendship" was the only way we could both know when he was double-timing us . . . we had to stay connected. Casper tried lots of things to disconnect me from Taz. He used things both of us said out of context to upset the other and create mistrust. But the more I got to know her, the less I actually felt comfortable being around her, having dated the same guy. I think because I sincerely liked her, it was just too difficult at that time to be constantly reminded of the pain we'd gone through. I really needed to just stop talking with her regularly because the stress of the situation was exhausting for me. So we did stop communications for a while. And the decision to isolate myself from her proved to be very dangerous indeed.

In September of 2000, Casper had convinced me again that he was "in process" of shutting things down with Taz, and that Snow White was preparing to move out of the house and in with a friend from school. I was spending lots of time with Casper and had promised to help him convince Taz nothing was going on between us other than the friendship. I agreed to this because he said he wanted to give her time to see we were actually close and our relationship wasn't just a physical thing. I felt horrible but understood his reasoning. I also wanted Taz to recognize that my relationship with Casper was very deep. Damn my ability to find a seemingly logical reason to justify Casper's actions! It was two months later when I discovered he was still sleeping with Taz, so I broke my promise to him and told her we'd been seeing each other behind her back. When the three of us got together to discuss it, he completely denied it and started to tell very ugly lies about me, right in front of my face. So I started to show Taz some of the pages he had been sending me as proof . . . and he actually told her I was crazy and sent them to myself! I was completely furious! I attempted to slap him, but he blocked my arm. So I threw a cup of water on him. It was a horrible scene that will forever embarrass me! Casper used this opportunity to convince Taz that I was an evil person who would stop at nothing to break them up. And after I acted like such an idiot, of course she believed him. I apologized to her, but she refused to believe I was telling the truth, and Taz and I did not speak for six months after that day. And I was quite relieved by that because I hated being in such a situation, and I certainly couldn't stand letting her think things were platonic between Casper and me when they were not. Looking back, I only wish I'd just walked away without telling her because all it did was cause tons of pain for us all.

Casper and I didn't speak at all for a month. Then he stopped by to apologize and make-up. Basically his story hadn't changed, "Snow White is moving out of the house, the relationship with Taz is in the process of ending." And of course, Snow White was still in the house, and he was still seeing Taz. Can you imagine that I still believed that story after everything that had transpired to this point? I can't. I was at least strongly committed to insuring our relationship remained platonic unless he shut down the others. I told him I'd rather hang onto our friendship and chalk the rest up to bad timing than be in a place of irreversible damage. I lasted in platonic mode until February 2001. A few months later, I found out Taz had never left his side and that he'd continued to escalate their relationship, despite promising to me it was over. And I know you are thinking, "Why can't she see this guy is just a dog?" But don't think that... it's so much more complex. The end result was the worst explosion Casper, Taz, and I ever had. The positive outcome was that I have now been able to completely free myself from any interest in a romantic relationship with Casper. I'm finally strong enough to be out of the fantasy and recognize all the deception for what it was. While Casper had most of the qualities I'd be looking for in my perfect match, he was missing that "core basic" ability to be honest! The truth is, I have to chalk this up to several bad choices by both of us. I'm responsible for my own actions and decisions... even if I made them based upon bad information. Because at some point, I really should have known better.

When I look at this logically, I have to ask myself how I could possibly have been so very clueless for this length of time. And of course, we know the honest truth is that I was stuck in the fantasy... not the reality. Casper is a Master of Deception... the M.O.D. It was easier to believe the lies than accept the reality that he had a wife, a girlfriend, and me... and who knows who else! What was it going to take for me to walk completely away from this situation? It should have been obvious to me that he would take action to bring these other relationships to a close if I were truly the one he wanted. But the many times I chose to walk away from him, he came back and asked for another chance. He would tell me he wouldn't be coming back if I wasn't the one he wanted. Despite the deception, I still believed some of his feelings might be sincere. I think Casper doesn't have the strength to be the one to end a relationship. And unfortunately, when faced with a difficult situation he simply couldn't avoid, his process was to lie . . . just like many of you guys! So my gut now says he really is a decent guy who married someone because he felt responsible for her, fell for a girl he couldn't be with long term but couldn't generate the strength to leave, and along the way he let me in more than he ever intended. I think of him like Tony Soprano, the primary character in the HBO series "The Sopranos". Tony has a wife he loves, a girlfriend he's crazy about, and a shrink he's captivated by. (In this scenario, I would be the shrink!) Maybe I believe this because my ego doesn't want to acknowledge I might have been "taken" to this degree . . . even though I do recognize deep inside that I might just be another chick he sleeps with on the side.

I know what you are all asking. "Weren't there signs? Didn't you suspect?" Of course there were. But remember, I was too busy living in my fantasy with Dream Casper to see the reality of M.O.D. Casper. And some people told me he was bad news, but I didn't listen. I always judge people for myself because I recognize that perceptions of others are not always accurate. So I will share with you some of the big signs I saw that should have told me Casper was in M.O.D. mode. And guys, I am sure that you will be laughing out loud because these are the completely obvious things that should really be plain as day. When I look back at this, it surprises me greatly that I got suspicious very early on, but I continued to ignore the huge red flags. I don't really know why it was all so easy to ignore. I think I was just so darn busy trying to be "understanding" since I had ended a marriage and know the complexities involved with leaving someone for whom you have deep feelings. So I allowed the obvious to just whip by. Okay, let's look at the list of those big things I should have seen.

Lesson Four

10 Huge Signs You Are Dealing with a Master of Deception (M.O.D.)

10. His "reputation" is legendary.
9. He is openly in a relationship while chasing you relentlessly.
8. His opening line to you is, "It is so important that you know I have never cheated on her, but you are the most amazing person I've ever met that it is SUCH an internal struggle for me."
7. His home phone number is unlisted and "off limits" to you until he "works through his issues" with the relationship he has to end.
6. His current girlfriend tracks him like the animal he is.
5. His sexual "technique" is so good it actually makes you nervous.
4. He is Mr. Mysterious when sharing details about routine activities.
3. He never actually commits to any activity with you, ever.
2. He disappears and reappears like the friendly ghost.
1. His smooth lines speak volumes over the whisper of his actions.

Ok, let's take these one at a time and wonder together why on earth I allowed myself to stay in this deal so long! The reputation should have been an indicator. Every guy that knows him thinks he is a "bad boy". I don't believe the philosophy that where there is smoke, there is fire. Honestly, people gossip about things that are not true every day. I stand by my rule to judge each person based upon my own experiences with him/her, and I strongly recommend that rule. And I still believe Casper is a decent guy who's made some really bad life choices. However, if you are dealing with someone who has the reputation of the century, at least keep your eyes wide open as you get to know each other! If guys think he is a bad boy, it is usually because they have either seen him in action or listened to him detail his conquests. And guys generally don't break the code of silence. It is part of being "in the club" to keep such activities under wraps. So, ladies, if your guy friends will actually tell you the man is a potential dog, PAY ATTENTION. One of my male buddies was trying to tell me this right from day one. In fact, every time something would happen he would send me a page spelling out dog on my pager. In fact, it got so bad so quickly that it progressed to "snoop doggy dog" because he needed more letters! It was funny, but he was right, and I should have been paying attention to my guy buddies. THEY KNOW. Ok, I must grovel now. To my guy buds who tried to tell me he was never leaving Snow White, and you know who you are, YOU WERE ALL RIGHT.

Ok, number nine, he's in a relationship and chasing you like there is no tomorrow. Don't misunderstand me. Again, I am the first to recognize falling for someone isn't something you plan or can control. And sometimes that person is already in a relationship when it happens. But the key difference I should have been looking at was the relentless pursuit. At first, this didn't develop naturally through a friendship over extended time. This happened with immediate flirtation over e-mail after meeting the guy once. For two straight months he sent me e-mail and pages every day, and I never made the first move. He was very determined. In fact, I didn't ever send the first daily communication until after the day he kissed me. It was obvious he was very interested. I just should have been asking myself exactly what he was interested in. I think I just needed the attention so badly because I had just dealt with all that pain of my marriage ending. Would someone who was sincerely thinking it was "fate" that we had met really have such a difficult time ending his relationship if he were seriously looking for something meaningful with me? My guy friends again say, "NO." He was telling me that Snow White was moving in with her mother when he was moving into his new house. Right up until the night before. You don't just plan a move the night before. I should have run the other direction at that very moment. But part of me is glad that I did not. I am certainly wiser now, and I'm thankful for that!

Number eight, the opening line. It was in one of his very first e-mails to me... how important it was to him that I understand he had never cheated on Snow White. I should have asked myself why he felt compelled to tell me this. It was too early for him to think he was going to be cheating with me! Was that the plan, to cheat with me? Was he trying to comfort me that I would be the first? Does a nice guy need to TELL you he's been faithful, or does he just need to SHOW you he's an upstanding person through his actions? We all know the answers to these questions, and I knew them back then. I was just smitten. And I did believe that he was going to leave her. He sounded sincerely unhappy in his relationship but appeared to genuinely care for her very much. And I mistook this as noble. And I'm a very intelligent woman. Go figure! I'm sure he does think about leaving Snow White sometimes... like a little freedom fantasy.

Number seven, the "off limits" phone number. It wasn't just that it was off limits in the beginning, he didn't lie about having a live-in girlfriend. It was that it never became "on limits". He did give me his number, but he asked me never to call him at home. If he were truly telling Snow White he wanted out, as he was telling me, she would not have been surprised that he was starting to pursue other women. And this takes us right on to number six. If the current girlfriend tracks him like a dog, he has probably displayed some level of bow wow behavior. She was obsessive with it, checked his voice mail *at work*, his e-mail *at work*, read his pages, monitored his every move. When I was married I never even opened a letter if it were just addressed to my husband. I trusted both of my husbands completely. I never felt an urge to check up on either of them. In fact, even through high school, I trusted My Cowboy completely. And we went to separate high schools! Snow White simply did not have a normal level of curiosity. And Casper cited this lack of trust as her problem, her chronic insecurity, and described it as one of their primary relationship issues. Of course, I now recognize that much of his behavior absolutely warranted her mistrust. But I do not understand why people stay in relationships without trust because it is such a basic element. It's one thing if you can forgive your partner and continue to trust, but to stay when there is NO trust??? Perhaps he felt her mistrust was justified because he knew he was behaving so badly. Maybe it was part of the entertainment value for him to see what he could actually slip past Snow White, Taz, and me. It's impossible to know what he was really thinking and why he did these things.

The sex was great, no doubt about number six. And I never thought I was just being used because we waited for a full year before actually crossing that line. I kept telling myself if he were just out to get laid, he would never have put in the effort. Think about it, he could have found plenty of willing partners with much less risk of being discovered. But there are times when I wonder if that was just part of his expertise because, honestly, the fact that we waited so long was the reason I felt he was just a confused nice guy. He knows how to make a girl feel as though she is important to him. He was such a great lover it made me nervous, and it seemed there was nothing Casper had not already experienced. He knew exactly what buttons to press. He was so attentive to how my body reacted to every touch, it was almost scary. And I am certain that he enjoyed taking me from the very conservative side of the board to a new sexual level. But I liked his "edginess" because I was ready for someone to help me stretch my sexual self. I think I was going through a stage most people experience much earlier in life. When I was younger, I guess I was just too busy being a "good girl" to be experimental. So this was an exploration for me, and I am still glad I had this experience with him no matter what because I have such a better understanding of myself now. And that is a positive thing. But it should have been clear to me that the great sex did not mean that I was special to him. (Again, I must refer you to lesson #5!) The entire time we were traveling, he always went back to his own room. He never spent the night with me from October until our Europe trip in April. One night I just broke down and told him how it upset me, and that I felt so cheap. He offered to stay. Of course I told him no because I wanted him to want to stay without prompting.

Mr. Mysterious, number four. He never gave details on the simplest of activities. If I started a conversation with, "So what are you up to today?" he would wonder exactly what I meant by the question. Honest guys don't have to wonder what ulterior motives you may have by asking innocent questions. He never shared what he was doing or where he was going. Even simple questions like, "Do you have a busy day planned?" were suspect. It was always vague statements like, "I need to take care of some things," or "I have to run an errand." He was always with "friends", never anyone specific. When simple things are secrets, there is probably a reason. Guys with nothing to hide do not show concern when you ask, "So how was lunch?" He also avoided detailed discussion about the situation. Casper would dodge a "talk" like the plague. And then when we would finally sit down to address the issues with the other women, I'd often get , "Let's not dwell on past events," or "I really don't want to get into the details." Yeah, we know why, don't we!

Number three, no firm plans. Guys who have nothing to hide can actually make firm plans with you. In the midst of deception, Casper could never commit to any activity. He could never actually commit to a plan, a time, nothing. He "might swing by later", or he would "try to get free", or he would "be in touch." He would never actually plan to go to lunch, to have dinner, or to share coffee. Everything was always up in the air with him, but I think he enjoyed the thought of me just sitting home waiting to see him. On the evenings that Snow White was out, he always let me know he might stop by, just so I would be there in case he wanted to. Even with the big things, like our trips, he was very noncommittal. The fact that he could not even commit to the travel should have been a big sign to me that something was up. As I look back at our trip to Europe now, I feel so stupid. The trip was originally scheduled in March. Two days before we were supposed to leave, he asked me not to join him, because too many people he worked with would be there. He didn't want to seem like a jerk for breaking his engagement and taking off with me. The reality is simply that Taz was planning go to Europe with her sister, so he couldn't have us both there. The day before he was to depart, his trip was postponed. When it was rescheduled for the first week of April, we planned to go together again. But remember, I waited to hear from him from Europe to see if he felt "up to company" after breaking his engagement before I joined him. And now I'm really not even certain he actually ended his engagement, much less what he was juggling before deciding he indeed wanted me in Europe. Are you as amazed as I am by all of this?

Number two, Casper my friendly disappearing ghost. I actually called him this name to his face. It became my nickname for him very early in our relationship. He would be in my life and then gone for no apparent reason. He would be back in my life just as suddenly. He would stop by my house and just kiss me for 10 minutes, then mysteriously he would "have to go". We would spend a great week together out of town, and the following week he would avoid me completely. He would ignore my pages, he would just be "busy" and not have time to even say hello. It was completely inexplicable. It felt like he was going through a constant internal tug-of-war. And hey, he probably was. I felt like his personal yo-yo. But someone who is convinced he wants to be with you to the point that he refers to his decision about your relationship as one for the "rest of his life" probably isn't going to demonstrate Casper-like behavior. There was never justification for this, and I should have seen it as a big clue that there were others in his life and he was purposely keeping me at a distance. But instead, I used this to support the "noble" character theory and was very impressed that it was so important to him to do the right thing and such a struggle to be with me until he made things right. How clueless I was to the reality . . . I must have written my chapter "live in the reality not the fantasy" but forgotten to read it!

Mercy! At any rate, it was his Casper behavior that I finally recognized as the single biggest indicator he was still seeing Taz. And unfortunately, every time my gut said, "Uh oh," it was right.

And finally, number one, actions speak louder than words. It is an absolutely true statement. I should have paid attention to the fact that his actions were only a whisper compared to the volume of his words. He was very consistent. He never took one action to show me that he was ready to actually be in a relationship with me. His words were beautiful... I motivated him to be more, I was unlike anyone else he'd met all his life, I was amazing, he didn't know what he'd do if he couldn't see my face some day. He said that this must be love, that it had taken him years to be able to say those words to Snow White, that he couldn't believe how strong his feelings for me were so quickly. Sometimes he'd even have tears in his eyes as he shared things with me and I never questioned the honesty of all those big statements. But I should have, because words are all I ever had, even if he meant those things at the moment he said them. There was no follow-up action to support those pretty words. Obviously he never ended either of his other relationships, which certainly should have been a huge sign. DUH. He told me for an entire year he was leaving Snow White. Then we had two really intense months together while traveling, only to be followed by his engagement. That should have been the baseball bat cracking down on my head. But no, I hung in there and believed his counselor story. And I look back and still don't know what things were true and what things were not. It wasn't the big huge deceptions that eventually sunk in, it was actually the lack of little actions that caught my attention. The fact that the first time I had knee surgery, he didn't even check to see if I was ok. The fact that he avoided spending most holidays with me. In fact, for my birthday in March 1999, just before Europe, he told me he might stay the weekend with me in Chicago to celebrate. So of course, I did not make other plans, but as usual he would not commit. So nature provided a gift. We had a huge snowstorm and his flight was cancelled. He could have stayed without any issue. He paged me to let me know he was going to be hanging out at the airport and I offered to come sit with him. I was willing to drive an hour through the blizzard just to have dinner. I asked him to call me to talk about it, and he would not. He just paged me with excuses... his cell phone battery had died, Snow White might find out if he used his calling card, etc. I gave him my calling card to use and still he wouldn't call me. Almost every flight was cancelled that night so he certainly could have stayed. If he cared, he would have at least picked up the phone. I often have a flashback of that night and remember that I have always been willing to fight a blizzard and he hasn't been willing to make a phone call to make this relationship happen. But of course, I always forgave him, and I still cannot believe that no matter how much my mind saw, my heart still had complete control. During our last few months, I was able to see the deceptions in progress because I finally began to recognize the times when his words and his actions did not match up.

Ladies, I hope you have read this chapter and realized that indeed some men can be incredibly devious. I know what you are all thinking, haven't I heard that guys will say anything to get laid????? In my wildest dreams, I never believed someone could be so intentionally deceptive. Even now, my heart wishes for a story that makes sense out of this. A story that shows he indeed had honorable intentions, but I know that is probably impossible. And guys, I hope you can see a tiny bit of the emotional impact these kinds of actions can have and will think long and hard before doing this to someone. I was so deeply hurt so many times. Taz was totally devastated on multiple occasions, and who knows what poor Snow White had to actually endure. It is hard to hear the words you want to hear and not believe them when you are in love. It's hard when everything feels so right for you to believe that the relationship can just be a game to the other person. I still ask myself how I believed so many of his lies for such a long time. I don't have a good answer to that question, except that my heart is stronger than my head! And as you know, I've still come through this hoping there's a good guy in there somewhere. But I can promise all of you that this will never happen to me again. Now, I want you to promise yourselves it will never happen to you! At the very least, I will never allow myself to again be treated with so little respect. I will pay attention to those small details that show whether someone cares for me, and I will remember that the M.O.D. is good at saying all the right things, but lousy at doing the right things. Next time I will watch the actions more closely than I will listen to the pretty words right from the start. And I will expect those actions to support those words and be consistent over a lengthy period of time. And most importantly, I will accept the things I see rather than conveniently ignoring obvious red flags. Casper hurt me so many times, there were so many depression shopping trips that I have to credit to his actions. It is almost scary to think about how much money I spent trying to give myself a lift! But I take responsibility for this, I allowed myself to be treated without the respect and kindness I deserve. I made my own decisions. I took my own actions. Heck, I actually enabled his behavior. However, on the positive side, I had some of the best sex of my life. I have greater detail on what to look for in a relationship now, and I have some fabulous new shoes! I'll even say that this whole experience has been somewhat fascinating. Remember, no matter how bad your situation, there always is a positive in there somewhere! Learn from your mistakes, find those positive factors, focus on them to gain some strength, and move relentlessly forward. Then never look back!

Chapter 6

Lesson Number Five

"Sex ≠ Love"

Ok, let me warn my female readers again. This just might be another chapter that causes severe inner turmoil for you. I have to break some difficult news. . . . sex and love are NOT the same. Guys, I know, you are all reading this saying, "DUH." But as you know, we ladies tend to equate the two things for some reason. Many of us tend to believe that once we have sex with you, we are "special" and the relationship has meaning. And of course, this is one of the things that scares you guys about having sex with us! Most of us girls just don't share that "separate" perspective you guys embrace, that mind-set that lets you view physical pleasure differently from emotional connection. It probably comes from all the "be a good girl" training we receive throughout our lives. And I'm not going to tell you ladies to drop this point of view, I'm just trying to point out that we should recognize that simply because two people decide to have sex doesn't mean deep feelings are there for both parties. I know it's a jagged little pill to swallow. But I promise, if you can recognize this key difference in the male/female perspective, you will enjoy a new level of sexual freedom. So go get a big glass of water and gulp this pill right down!

Hey folks, whoever said, "Sex isn't the most important thing," lied. It's absolutely a cornerstone factor in a successful relationship. And let me clarify . . . when I say sex, I mean all the wonderful physical connections that enhance the intimacy between two people, from a simple touch or kiss on down the line. When you stay physically connected to your partner, you have a distinct advantage for making your relationship last. It's one of the things that helps you continue to grow closer. It's one of the things that keeps your partner interesting. And, it's one of the things that keeps energy in the relationship. The challenge is keeping things sexually creative enough to keep your relationship electrically charged for a lifetime. And that's why swallowing that jagged little pill and understanding men and women have different perspectives on the issue of sex is so critically important.

Barbara DeAngelis wrote in one of her books that women need to have emotional feelings to have sex, and men need to have sex to have access to their emotional feelings. I think she is 155% right on target. It is difficult for most women I know to believe that men and women view sex differently, but like I said, I think it is something we all must accept if we want a fabulous relationship. Ladies, you have to understand how important sex is to your man if you want to insure a long-term monogamous relationship. So please recognize the fact that sex is a huge driver in a relationship for guys. It's just part of their wiring. Understand it, and don't hold it against them. Guys, by the same token, you must understand what things women must feel to be able to give you the sex you are looking for. There is a confidence we ladies need to have in our relationship to be capable of having sex at a level that will interest you guys indefinitely. Remember when we looked at the differences between men and women? Remember that you cannot expect everyone to have the same perspective as you? This is just another classic area where there is a critical difference in how we view a very important issue. So dramatically different in fact that the issue gets it's own chapter! Again, neither perspective is right or wrong, but we must recognize the difference to enhance the chance for long-term relationship success.

I think because sex has such emotional significance to many women, it seems really difficult to "reduce it" to a physical act of pleasure. It makes it seem cheap if we take away the emotional significance. But really, we don't have to take away that significance to understand this other point of view. Remember ladies, just because we can acknowledge that sex is also about physical pleasure doesn't mean we still can't choose to only share that pleasure with someone we love! This is the perspective that I chose to adopt to allow myself to go places physically I'd never gone before. We are taught from day one that "good girls" only have sex with the man they love. Think about it . . . historically premarital sex was such a tabu. A guy wanted his wife to be a virgin. The white wedding dress was a symbol of the woman's purity. A girl who had sex with more than a few partners was considered a serious slut, and the "double standard" on this is still alive and well. And these are just a few of those archaic viewpoints. Ok, perhaps "traditional viewpoints" would be a more politically correct phrase. But our culture has changed so much over the past twenty years in its perceptions and attitudes about sex. Now we have shows like HBO's "Sex and the City" with a cast member to represent each of the many female sexual viewpoints out there today. At one extreme is Amanda, the woman who perceives sex as a simple act of physical pleasure she can never get enough of. At the other is Charlotte, who is always looking for Mr. Prince Charming and demonstrating a very traditional perspective. There are many great books encouraging women to better understand their own sexuality and power. Yet somehow, many women still have not made it to the level of separation between sex and emotion that many men seem to have always had. It's not a bad thing. It's not a good thing. It is simply something we must all remember if we want to be conscious of those differences that inhibit our relationships from working at their best.

In my first three relationships, I really believed sex wasn't a core driver. I was wrong. I look back on all three of them and can clearly see that when the sex started to dwindle, the relationship was also beginning to fizzle. And I'm sure that when issues begin to arise, it has an impact on the sex. But what is really the cause, and what is really the effect? Is it lack of sex that results in a lack of interest and, therefore, allows other issues to appear increasingly important? Or, is it those other issues that drive a wedge between two people and result in a relationship that has lost some of its closeness . . . and therefore some of its sexual energy? I'm certain it must be a combination of both, but I'll go out on a limb here and say that I now believe sex to be a cornerstone of a solid relationship. It's absolutely a baseline fundamental. And I believe the reason is pretty simple. Physical intimacy places this relationship on a level that's different from all the other relationships in our lives. (This assumes you are not having multiple sexual relationships!) Sex can connect you on a highly intimate level, and when all of the right things are in place for the practical aspects of the relationship, magic happens! I now understand that two people who can maintain their physical passion have a total edge on the rest of us. It is one of the things that can keep you close enough to see you through tough times. It is one of those things that can launch you to a higher place most couples don't achieve. Passion truly just brings another level of closeness to a relationship. Without an intimate physical connection, what exists is simply an amazing friendship.

But regardless of what sex means to each of us, it is certainly something that is uniquely important to us all. And I say it is a core element for a solid relationship because it gives us a level of access to our partner we cannot maintain without it. There are so many books that deal with how to bring passion back into the relationship. Why do we find it a challenge to keep our relationships sexually charged? Doesn't the passion seem to come so easily in the beginning? Every encounter seems to escalate to a new level as you get to know each other both physically and emotionally.

How does it slip from the stage of dying to rip each other's clothes off to mere routine? We let it... we stop paying attention to it... that's how.

When I look back at my first three relationships, and then I compare them with Casper, I can see patterns I want to insure I never allow to happen again. With My Cowboy, Mr. Porsche, and The Exec, things were fine in the beginning. I used to flirt with each of them like mad during the early stages of the relationships. But in each case, as time passed, I stopped really making a conscious effort to turn them on. And then they stopped trying to turn me on. Even the simple things, like flashing a hot little smile over dinner, have an incredible impact on keeping the passion alive. All those little flirty actions can truly keep a level of interest that is otherwise impossible to maintain, because flirting is all about paying a special level of attention to your partner. And in every one of my past relationships, when the physical connection began to slip, the level of emotional intimacy in the relationship began to falter. And then the parts of the relationship that were less than perfect began to get increased attention. More focus was placed on the things that were going wrong than on the positive aspects of the relationship, regardless of how many positive aspects were still there. Because there is such a feeling of great closeness from being physically connected to someone special, if that closeness starts to slip, I think perhaps we start over-analyzing the relationship to identify the cause. And this puts too much focus on all those issues that used to seem so small. Face it folks, you will find what you look for if you look hard enough. If you focus on the positives, you will see them. If you focus on the negatives, you will find them as well. And when you become consumed by the negative energy, your desire to have a physical connection decreases accordingly. It's a vicious cycle! So my first pattern I won't repeat is to stop flirting. I will be committed to the quick flash of a mischievous smile, a whisper of a seductive thought, and an attitude that will drive my guy crazy ***EVERY*** day. Not to mention wearing deadly shoes that will insure he wants to rip my clothes off upon sight!! Girls, flirt with your honey like mad and put effort into how you look. If he's the love of your life he's worth the effort.

My Cowboy and I were both young and inexperienced lovers. A big part of the excitement for me always came from the way he kissed me. We used to just sit and kiss for hours. But over time, we kissed less and less before sex, which left me feeling a bit less connected. In fact, this was a fundamental problem for me. Personally, I now understand that I need the passion of great kisses to feel connected enough to have sex. It's one of the few things that can honestly shut down my brain, the right kiss will completely take me over. In the movie "Pretty Woman", Julia Roberts in character as a prostitute states that she will do anything with a man except kiss because it is just too personal. I guess I am just one of those believers in the power of the kiss. One of my past mistakes was in not just driving that action myself. Certainly I don't have to wait for my love to kiss me! I should have just been the one to insure that powerful affection continued, but I was too busy being "old fashioned". And so the second pattern I won't repeat is waiting for my love to be the initiator of the kiss, or anything else I want to enjoy! As my connection to My Cowboy started to slip, things just were not the same. Have you ever been at a point in your relationship where things just don't feel the same and you don't know why? It just kind of sneaks up on you . . . that physical distance. I think that moment can be a defining one in your future. It's a time when a "physical reconnection" is required to help bring the relationship back on track. It is entirely possible to successfully repair a disconnected relationship if the right ingredients are there. The most important ingredient is a mutual desire to fix things coupled with some substantial effort in raising your passion bar.

It's funny how simple isolated actions can completely shape our attitudes about sex. At the rocky end of my relationship with My Cowboy, he came to my apartment one night in a drunken rage. In fact, he pounded on the door so hard that the apartment number fell off. I will never forget that night. He was trying to win me back and let's just say he would not take no for an answer! No,

I'm not suggesting he tried to rape me. He just wouldn't stop kissing me and didn't listen to anything that I said. Here was someone I loved deeply who was just too drunk to realize that I really didn't want to go there. I could have given him a hard no, gotten ugly, and made him leave. But I loved him and that wasn't what I wanted to do. I knew the fastest way out was to just let it happen. So I did. But I wish I had not, and that night honestly has haunted me for many years. I don't know why . . . it was a very simple thing we'd done a million times! The next day, he could barely remember we'd been together because he had been so drunk. After the break up, he would call me in the middle of the night because he was in so much pain. When I finally asked him to please stop, he did immediately. But the whole experience really changed me. I felt so bad that I hurt him so deeply. I think I felt afraid to be sexy because I might cause too much pain if things didn't work. And this was the start of my own sexual withdrawal.

With both my marriages to Mr. Porsche and The Exec, it was really hard for me to feel sexually free anymore. In fact, The Exec told me he thought I was completely afraid of my sexuality. I see now that he was right. Both relationships started out great. But both relationships suffered very early physical disconnections for very similar reasons, although different circumstances. I knew very quickly that my marriage to Mr. Porsche was in jeopardy, probably within the first six months. Because our life desires were just so different, very quickly we began to argue about big things. Nothing I did seemed to get his approval. He could not control me and I constantly frustrated him. It was just a sad state. We spent very little time together. He worked all day, then spent evenings in our garage working on race car parts for his start-up business. When you don't spend quality time together to stay emotionally connected, it's very difficult to keep the desire for physical intimacy, particularly for women. So within six months, our sexual activity had slipped to such infrequency it was a shame. In fact, it happened so infrequently that I barely remember even having sex with Mr. Porsche. The Exec and I were very emotionally and mentally connected, but travel to opposite sides of the globe started eating away at our opportunities to be with each other. I think it is virtually impossible to maintain an intimate relationship with someone if you constantly spend time apart. Slowly, as we spent less time together, and as I became lonelier, I became less interested in having sex with The Exec. Those feelings of "he doesn't miss me" because he wasn't "paying enough attention to me" before and after his trips made me feel unloved. When our video business was failing, he felt less connected to me. Both of us became physically disconnected, and he also became emotionally disconnected. I guess the demise was only a matter of time. But when I recognized what was happening, I tried to give us that "reconnection", and I believed our relationship was completely fixable. But it was too late for him and he was not interested in any solution except an ending. And it is critical to recognize that if only one of you wants to fix the relationship, it is time to let go and walk away. It is impossible to repair a relationship without both parties taking some action. And so I can tell you that spending too much time separated from the man I love will be the third pattern I won't repeat.

I am only beginning to understand the sexual part of myself. Casper was a great help to me in this area. He is a highly experienced lover. I doubt there is anything he hasn't already done, and he is very clear about the importance sex plays in his relationships. I had a level of physical desire for Casper like I had never experienced before. It was such frenzied lust! And he was just a deadly kisser. I have an absolute weak spot for a guy who can make me go dizzy with one kiss. Trust me when I tell you I could lip lock with him and never come up for air! No matter what else happened, I give Casper the credit for helping me find my sexual self. Very healthy for me, it had just been an aspect I'd left locked away and unexplored for all this time. He was a GREAT lover! For a while I was so intimidated by his skill that I was constantly in fear of my own performance. It was so silly. I was afraid that I wasn't being sexy or adventurous enough, even though it was pretty clear the lust was mutual. He even told me it was the best sex he'd ever had, but I was never really sure those weren't just more "great words". I recognized how important it was to stay physically connected with Casper even though we spent time apart. I realized that the physical connection we shared was unique, at least for me, and I wanted to see what I could do to enhance it and keep it growing. That was part of the reason I began the virtual pager sex game. It would have been impossible to continue a relationship long distance without some level of physical connection, so we just made a game of escalating fantasies. They started very romantic, and eventually became completely graphic. It's funny . . . for a long time I could send things to his pager that I could never say in person. It was almost an anonymous feeling, just getting to write the words and launch them. It was such a "safe" format. I would think of exotic and unusual places for us to be together. Then I would craft an imaginary little story and describe what we would do to each other in the most intimate level of detail. Mental fantasies would always make us crazy for each other!! I'm sure this is why so many people are having virtual sex on the Internet!

Those little pager fantasies allowed me to become less afraid to feel sexy and to show him I was feeling sexy. And knowing that nothing I could do would be a surprise to Casper, I just wasn't worried that he was ever going to think I wasn't a "nice girl". After all, he participated in the transformation! I knew I could explore with him free of judgment. So I was able to start getting creative with our sex, and I was able to enjoy a whole new attitude. It was terrific! There was something about the way he communicated with me during our intimate times that made me feel completely at ease. I wish I could tell you what it was, but I can't isolate any specific comments or actions. I can just tell you that everything . . . his tone of voice, his choice of words, the way he touched me, and the look in his eyes all said, "This is our special thing." Sorry, I'm not going to share all the juicy details except to tell you that I paid attention to what turned him on, then tried to think of ways to enhance it. Oh don't be frustrated. It's really none of your business! All I can tell you is that I've never had such a blast! But let me give you a few ideas to spur your creative thoughts. Men are very visually stimulated creatures, so why don't you place several mirrors all the way around your bed so he can watch no matter what the angle. You might find it to be incredibly erotic! Or why don't you try blindfolding him, and bring in a tray of tasty condiments, ranging from whipped cream to warm chocolate sauce. Play with a wide variety of different textures and temperatures. While he is blindfolded, drizzle them and suck them from . . . well use your imagination . . . then kiss him with a little on your tongue and make him guess the condiment! Or try some lighting effects, like a strobe! Sometimes very simple things, like a flashing light that makes you a little dizzy, can be the greatest seductive tools! I was able to view my physical time with Casper as a special playtime, the most special playtime two people in love could share. And so I no longer felt the need to "behave", and I started to enjoy complete sexual freedom. No matter what happens in my future, one of the things I hope will never change is having this playful, lighthearted attitude regarding sex. My last pattern I will not repeat . . . thinking sex is about anything but fun!

I used to think sex had to be a very serious, very romantic, very meaningful experience and nothing else. I needed the lights off, the "right" environment, meaningful discussion afterwards. But my perspective has changed so dramatically. Not in every sense . . . I still believe the choice to be with someone physically is best when the person is very important to you. I could never be so personal and so free with someone I wasn't mad about! And I'd have to develop the right level of trust in my relationship before I'd be ready to cut loose. But now I think the actual physical time together should be about having fun! I think it is an opportunity to make your partner feel good in a way you share with no one else, and it is something that should be lighthearted, not something that creates pressure for you both. I can honestly tell you that sadly there were some points in my various relationships that I completely dreaded the thought of having sex. What a shame!

Sex is the most unique opportunity you have to connect with each other, a more personal than anything else you can do for each other. It is so important to understand each other physically, to be able to grow with each other as you learn what makes your partner feel fabulous. Isn't it fun to have the opportunity to make someone you care for deeply feel incredible? So, personally, I don't equate sex with love anymore, but I certainly don't want to experience this kind of pleasure unless I'm with someone I have very special feelings for. In fact, I think for me to maintain this level of freedom, I need a high level of trust in my partner and confidence in our relationship. And I am so glad that I have had the opportunity to re-evaluate this for myself. Casper, thank you for this one!!

There are some very important things that you guys and gals must remember if you want to have a great physically charged relationship. Guys, for most of us ladies, there must be a high level of trust in our relationship to truly "cut loose" sexually. We need to feel completely safe with you. We must know that there will be no "judgment" if we suggest something sexually creative. It's important that we can be confident you will still think of us as a nice girl. We must not have any concern that you'll go give the intimate details to your buddies. (Even though we probably think it's ok to tell our girlfriends!) We need you to let us grow into this at our own pace . . . we cannot feel pressured in this area. For most of us, we won't even know how to discuss this with you . . . and you probably don't know how to broach it with us either! So, this means that someone just has to be brave and take action.

Gals, I recommend that you be the ones to step up to the plate and initiate the creativity. I know you don't want to hear that. But your guy is just as concerned that you'll think he has some secret past if he really tells you everything he wants. So, until you get to a mutually comfortable creative place . . . ladies, just be the driver so you can progress at whatever pace makes you comfortable. It's important to give your relationship a physical punch EVERY day. Relax, I'm not telling you that you have to have sex every day. Although, by all means, feel free! I'm saying take one action each day to keep him interested. Squeeze his buns, nibble his ear for just a second, or lift your skirt as he's walking out the door and give him a quick glimpse of your sexy panties (and wear them frequently). Call him at work and whisper something wickedly seductive on the phone. You don't even have to say something edgy to be seductive. Just whisper, "I want you . . . RIGHT NOW!" Yes girls, if you want him to stay interested, you must take some actions to keep him attracted. You wouldn't let a day pass without talking to him, would you? This is no less important than conversation. Think of this as "body talk". Do yourselves a favor and remember that your relationship is worth one hot action every day. I promise, your payback will be tenfold!

I know it sounds a little intimidating, attempting to find something steamy to do each day. Don't be afraid. You can do this. Ladies, I'm talking about really easy stuff here . . . you don't have to do anything more than look at his manly parts with a sinful little smile. Yes, I realize I'm talking about making effort *every* day, and that is time consuming. But trust me, your relationship needs this energy if it's going to last. And you can either accept that fact, or deal with the consequences that come from lack of sexual charge. It's really a small effort in the big picture, don't you think? And guys, you've got to be a contributor . . . play back! Kick in some romantic creativity! Reward our efforts with a rose or two! If you don't respond with positive reinforcement, we'll get a little spooked and probably give up pretty quickly!

So from this chapter, I hope you will take away the importance of passion in the relationship. When you are early in the relationship and are doing all those little things that bring you close, keep a little list of things that turn your partner on, and I mean those things that make you both want to have sex in the first place. The way you look at each other, things you do for each other, how you flirt with each other, and the time you'll reserve for each other, etc. These are the things you cannot stop doing. They are the things you cannot neglect, and that you have to reach for if the physical connection does start to dwindle. Always focus on the positive parts of your relationship. Remember all the reasons you are lucky to be with this person when you go to sleep at night. Be thankful for having someone special in your life. Spend time together. Continue to date even if you are married. Constantly look for new ways to enjoy each other, both mentally and physically. Don't take your special relationship for granted, because it's a rare gift. You are lucky to have your partner, so cherish him or her. Remember that a significant part of your relationship power will come from the passion, and passion is only possible when you spend time together. Sit down right now and think of five things you can do differently to bring that sexual energy back into your relationship. If you both do this, you will have a new sexual adventure every week for the next two and a half months! Hey, if it's too uncomfortable to discuss your ideas, write them down, put them in a bowl, and draw them at random . . . no discussion required! My own mistakes I will not repeat are to stop flirting, to wait for my guy to be the initiator when there's something I want, to spend too much time away from my guy, and to think sex is about anything but FUN! Now make sure you don't make those mistakes! While sex and love are not the same, both the emotional feelings and the physical pleasure are requirements for a lasting relationship.

Chapter 7
___

Lesson Number Six

Give Good "C"

The "C" word. Communication. Don't underestimate its power. Strong communication can make you an untouchable duo. Lack of communication can force you back to the land of singles! And when I say communication I don't just mean words, I mean relating to each other on verbal, emotional, and physical levels. The need for good "C" is yet another lesson I learned during the departure of The Exec from my life. It's funny... if you had asked me while we were married, I'd have told you we had great communication. But when The Exec and I were separated, I started to recognize that our communication process was really weak, and I wanted to understand why. As we went through the difficult process of ending our relationship, it became more and more clear that The Exec just did not understand most of what I was saying, and that I really had to work to understand him. It was exhausting! So I started to write him letters to eliminate the obstacles we created when we talked. This made things more clear for him. It was the only way I could remove the emotion from the discussion and provide enough detail for him to understand me, without causing him to feel the need to generate a counter point for every sentence out of my mouth! And as I look back, I see that the root cause of our communication challenge was actually pretty simple. It was a direct result of the big three differences between men and women. I was focused on the big picture, building the whole story to make my point. He was instantly ready for the point, so he perceived every detail that came out of my mouth as I built the story to be the end point. And as many guys do, he had a counter point for each of those minor details, so we ended up arguing before I had ever raised the real issue. By writing to him, I could go back and edit out unnecessary details to make my communications much more direct. At the time, I didn't understand these dynamics. But I did recognize that I needed to keep my letters crisp and direct to help him understand my perspectives. Wow, to learn how to edit myself like this during conversation is certainly on my list of things to do!

I think if you can master strong communication as a couple, you have locked up 50% of the formula for success. If you think about building a solid relationship like building a house, good "C" is the frame on the foundation of intimacy. Yes, I'm saying again that the other 50% is that "intangible" quality, that amazing level of chemistry you should never even start dating without, that emotional and sexual energy we talked about in the last chapter. I'm saying these factors are equal in importance, and I'm convinced that a full 100% is required to enable a relationship to go the distance and keep you happy along the way. You have to have both a foundation and a frame to construct a house! And when you think about it, after foundation and frame, much of the rest is just decorative! I'm suggesting that the emotional and physical intimacy serves as the foundation because it is often easier to first establish the right feelings. Those intimate feelings arise quickly! It is much more challenging to put a solid communication process in place. Yeah right, if I know this stuff and it is really this easy, why don't I have a successful relationship myself? Obviously because it has taken me 36 years and a lot of learning the HARD WAY to figure it out!

Communication is more than just exchanging words. It's about really listening and understanding each other, sharing your dreams, experiences, fears, and your honest opinions. Communicating is about really letting each other "in". Speaking through your eye contact and your touch. Feeling emotionally and intellectually charged. It sounds simple enough, but it is actually a very challenging aspect in a long-term relationship. In the beginning, communicating seems so easy. As you are caught up in the chemistry those words seem to flow quickly as you get to know each other. And of course, when you are just getting to know each other, there is so much to discuss! You can talk for long periods of time, yet still manage to stay guarded and safe. In a new relationship, everything is about discovery. The complications don't become visible until much later! One of the reasons communicating grows harder is because you become completely vulnerable to another human when you are really open. Think about it . . . you are giving unlimited access to your most personal self.

When the newness fades, when you have gone through the basic information about each other's lives, you must progress to a deeper level of communication to advance your relationship beyond the surface level. I think lots of people never make it past surface level communication and have surface level relationships as a result. You know what I'm talking about . . . they get through the baseline information exchanges, learn the history, and get to a nice comfortable level of daily "updates". They give a brief summary of the work day, family status, and plans for dinner. You've probably all experienced this level of communication. It's simply going through the motions of the day, and it keeps you somewhat connected, but doesn't do much to progress the relationship. I think many people are actually comfortable in this place and do not even recognize they need a high level mental "connection" to be happy and fulfilled. But I also think this is what makes so many people vulnerable to affairs, because they are not connected to their partners on a level that is robust enough to eliminate the feelings of "missing something". And I believe this is actually one of the contributing factors to sex becoming more of a routine than a driving force in your relationship. (Remember again lesson #5!) When your mental connection starts to fizzle, the sex seems to just become a little less interesting. It truly seems to me that a high level mental connection is part of keeping a relationship fully charged and continuously intriguing. And I suspect that lack of mental chemistry in our primary romantic relationship is why the office is so frequently the source of affairs. Mental energy balances the sexual energy, and when you have both the relationship can have amazing depth.

Without the mental intrigue, the chemistry goes flat over time. The combination of both these types of connections is rare, but when it happens, it's almost indestructible! And this is precisely why my relationship with Casper was always so darn deadly . . . having both the mental punch and the sexual burst. He had the most brilliant mind of anyone I've ever met, and I've always been both fascinated and entertained by our discussions. It's just a riot to sit and chat with him, and that is a big factor for me in a relationship. I need a strong mental charge! It's important to be realistic with yourself and understand what kind of communication level you require so you can find the right partner.

It's a shame that many people go through relationships without the intimacy that can be achieved with a high level of communication. Personally, I find it hard to imagine going through life with someone who does not know my every dream, could not anticipate my every thought, wouldn't spend time to listen, wasn't with me in spirit every step of the way. And I want and need to understand all those things about my partner as well. But how on earth can we accomplish this level of understanding about each other? It's tough. You must be completely open and honest with each other. You must be a great listener and must be able to listen without judgment because these are the elements that build trust. Trust is another fundamental factor if you want a relationship to last a lifetime. In the "relationship house", consider trust to be the walls constructed on your frame of communication. Complete trust is a very difficult thing because it makes you emotionally vulnerable.

It is hard to leave yourself totally exposed to another person, even if that person is your life partner. But you have to take the risk if you want to achieve that ultimate level of intimacy, and I certainly believe it is worth it. I know so many people who are able to protect themselves from this level of vulnerability, who have safety walls they have built that keep people from getting too close. I do not know how to do that, to turn off my emotions and keep people out. Sometimes I wish that I did, and I always wish that I could at least understand this process. I am simply a wide open book. It is easy to get to know me, and it is easy for me to quickly become close with people. I do not know how to control my feelings, to shut them off. Are feelings really controllable? Certainly you can distract yourself from the feelings. You can focus on work or other things to keep busy, but how do you just eliminate them?

Casper seemed to be completely capable of controlling his feelings. When I watched him dealing with his relationship situations, it was apparent that he was able to keep me and everyone else at a distance whenever he desired. Whenever we took a few steps closer, it seemed he would purposely push us backwards. He wasn't able to do this if we were together, he had to disappear and stop spending time with me to create that distance. Remember this process was actually the cause of his nickname... Casper. He would simply disappear and detach, stop spending any time with me, and stop talking to me. And when his feelings were back in control, he would reappear. I am not sure if he was just trying to manage the speed of the relationship, or the level of connection, or just being the M.O.D. Maybe it's a combination of the three. At any rate, it always succeeded in disconnecting us to a degree. Remember, when you do create distance in your communication, it takes a toll on your relationship.

Having a good communication process can help you work through the most difficult of times. If you are able to really listen to each other, you can craft a solution to whatever situation is at hand. Without the ability to listen, you have the potential for unnecessary misunderstandings and frustrations. It is very easy to only see things from your own perspective. How can you craft a solution without understanding both points of view? I hate to break it to you, but your personal perspective is not always right! I think the hardest time to be a good listener is when you are upset and strong emotions are involved. And remember, because we each use our own beliefs and experiences to develop our perspectives, we can never assume our partner's will be the same. In fact, if our perspectives were the same, would there ever be conflict? Of course not, we would always be in agreement! And I'm sure living life without other interesting perspectives would get boring rather quickly! Remember that men and women are different. Typically we speak a different language and certainly have different points of view. The trick is to both understand each other's perspective, and to work together to come to a common solution.

A complicating factor is that men and women typically have different styles of communication. And the difference in communication styles is clearly evident at a very young age. Once I led a great research project for my company to help understand kids and their communication process. It was a study in the ways girls and boys from ages 8-16 communicate with each other. The boys were typically very direct in their communications and limited the discussion to "facts". They talked about the football game, the movie, traded details about where to meet to play. They made and kept friends not through communication, but by "doing stuff" together. The girls talked about feelings, emotions, their reactions to everything going on in their lives, not just the facts about those events. They made and kept friends with conversation. The boys were much more brief in their communications, much less emotional, a pure information exchange at its best. The girls discussed their feelings for very long periods of time and communicated with lots of detail. It was absolutely fascinating to watch this dynamic happening before my own eyes! Even at this early age, guys tend to be brief and factual, women more detailed and emotional in communications. So again, it's important to recognize there's no right or wrong way to communicate, but you have to pay attention to your partner's communication process if you want to insure a successful relationship.

So how can we communicate effectively if we are so different? How can we relate on a very deep level if we do not even speak the same language? Isn't that a million dollar question? There's no easy answer, but I think it starts with understanding yourself, like we discussed earlier. It is impossible to really relate to someone else when you do not understand yourself. Do you understand what is really important to you in life? Do you understand what makes you tick? Do you know why you are feeling the way you feel about your relationship right now? Big questions aren't they! Once you have a clear understanding of yourself, you need that same understanding of your partner to communicate intimately. It's work to honestly get to know your partner! It's hard enough just to really understand yourself. But it is essential to understand what makes your partner happy, sad, nervous, upset, excited, etc. to be really close. Do you know right now what things are really important to your partner? You can learn these things by closely paying attention to him/her every day. Pay close attention, all the time, and watch how your partner reacts to different situations each day. It is critically important to learn these things about each other, then to always keep them in mind.

It's funny how I wasn't able to really understand The Exec until he left me. During the year we were separated, when I tried to pull us back together, I really paid attention to everything he did and how he reacted to different situations. I finally saw that he was one who needed tremendous reinforcement to feel secure. It seemed he was in need of approval for everything he did. During our marriage, I was often frustrated by his need to "wear" his accomplishments and possessions publicly. For example, when people would come to our house, he would tour them around and point out the "best stereo" on the market, and the "most expensive" this, and the "most exclusive" that. It frustrated me, because I like to be a little more humble, and I felt he was making our friends feel uncomfortable. What I wish I had recognized was that The Exec was just in need of outside validation that he was "making it" in life. His childhood was a financial struggle. It took our divorce for me to really see and understand how important money was to him and understand why. I had no idea money was a core driver for him and that our financial perspectives were totally different the entire time we were married. Perhaps if I had been able to see this about him earlier, I would have reacted to things differently and would have given him the approval and support he so desperately needed. Or even better, I might have recognized that we would have never had similar priorities on this major issue, and would have never started dating him!

I think I did a much better job communicating while getting to know Casper. I tried really hard to understand him when we began our friendship. I worked to be a great listener, and to avoid making any judgments. It was important to me to try and honestly see his point of view. One of the reasons I allowed myself to get back into a romantic relationship with him so many times was the strength of our communication process. We had many long conversations about both his relationships. He seemed to be experiencing so many of the things I had experienced while struggling to end my previous relationships. There were times I felt I knew him so well, and sometimes we were both a little spooked by my ability to know exactly how much space he needed, or what he was going to say. I thought Casper and I were similar in many ways. I thought we both had the ability to give up our own desires to make someone else happy. It seemed that he agonized over leaving Snow White just as I had mentally tortured myself when divorcing Mr. Porsche. I thought we both had great depths of emotion. Though he was able to shut his emotions down at will, there appeared to be so many moments when he displayed great emotional insight with what he said. Despite the fact that we both communicated a pretty firm set of "life rules", we both broke them frequently. I thought having a great relationship was the most important part of life for each of us because he put so much time into his relationship with Snow White. It's hard to feel that you know someone as well as I felt I knew Casper, only to have doubt cast across your entire relationship.

Through our communication process, I also saw some key differences I believed could have an impact if Casper and I ever had a relationship together. I make very quick decisions. I look at the pros, the cons, the risks of each, and then I go for it and never look back. And I do all of that in about five minutes on the most major life decisions! Casper demonstrated that same kind of decision process, but did it over lengthy periods of time. And once he made a decision, he would re-evaluate it over and over again. I think another core difference was that Casper seemed to need "public opinion" on his side. He appeared to care very much about whether or not people would think he was a bad person. In fact, I do believe a core driver behind many of his lies was the fact that he didn't want to create the impression that he was a bad guy. It even seemed to be part of his struggle in leaving both Snow White and Taz. It looked as if he needed to do "what was right" just as much as what he wanted. I could really care less what people think of me. I never make a choice and wonder what the reaction of my friends will be. Sometimes I worry if I will feel like a bad person, but never if others will think poorly of me. If Casper and I were ever a couple, I would have to be capable of recognizing these differences are just part of who he is, and not allow myself to be frustrated by these differences. I would have to be capable of giving him the space he needed to go through his own processes without pressuring him to do it my way or at my pace. Many things happened between us on our roller coaster affair, and I admit now that I'm not sure who he really is. Casper has certainly had a "colorful" past. What I thought I saw was a man capable of very deep feelings, who had a very mature perspective, and was an amazing and rare person. I thought Casper might be capable of the kind of love I knew I would need to have in my life. I just thought he didn't recognize how to capitalize on his own positive abilities. But he certainly had mastered using the negative ones to their full potential! And Casper and I would have never made it as a couple if he wasn't able to open up and be honest rather than avoiding issues and telling lies!

If you can master truly getting to know each other, the next hurdle is to create a common language you can both understand. Sad, but true, the languages of men and women are different. It amazes me that we have such a tough time accepting that fact. But to have a successful relationship, we must master the ability to speak in a way that our partner will understand. And this includes language beyond words. I saw a very funny comedy show called "Defending the Caveman" in which the star, Rob Becker, points out that women are simply blessed with more words than men, and when guys don't want to talk anymore, it's just because they have run out of words! Remember from lesson #1 that relationships are a core driver for women, and communicating verbally is part of how we build those relationships. Guys don't need to talk like we do. They express themselves differently. They relate through action and bond through activity. Even as kids, boys go play while girls talk on the phone.

So for successful communication, what are the options? We can either learn to speak our partner's language, or we can create a joint language we both understand. Or, we can do some creative combinations of the two. In any case, we have to keep these things in mind when we are trying to make sense to each other. Then we must always remember those big three differences we covered in lesson #1. If we can remember the ways we are different, we can begin to learn how to relate. Our differences impact the way we speak and the way we listen. I read once that you would never expect a puppy to understand your words. You use things like tone of voice, physical touch, and yummy treats to teach the puppy. You are perfectly happy that the puppy starts to slowly learn your language. You don't get mad when the puppy doesn't understand you at first. And you understand that it is a process that develops over time. You have to remember that, just like a puppy, your partner does not speak your language, and patient teaching is required if you want to be able to communicate.

At my company there was a great training program that talked about culturally sensitive communications for business. We looked not only at the issue of different languages in different countries, but the different communication styles that are present within different cultures. And we looked at the fact that there are many cultures, based on gender, age, religion, geography, etc. Our instructor talked about two primary communication styles . . . linear and circular. Linear communication is just that, from one point directly to the next, straight to the issues. Circular communication takes a more roundabout path, talking through more detail and more process to develop the big picture. We learned in the class that men are typically linear communicators, while women are typically circular communicators. I really watch for this style to show itself when I communicate with people. It helps me communicate better in business and in my personal relationships. By paying close attention to different people in discussions, I can see that it is possible to speak and listen in different communication styles. I try to speak in the style that the other person hears. I try to listen in the style of the other person's speech. So if someone is a linear speaker and a circular listener, I listen in linear style and speak in circular style. I cannot tell you how just having this awareness has enhanced my own communications, both personally and professionally.

Ok, I know this is really easy to say and difficult to execute. So let's look at some practical examples. Take one of my former bosses at work. He is a circular communicator, but a very linear listener, which is a fancy way to say he gives lots of detail on the way to his point, but doesn't want the details when listening to someone else! He is a very traditional guy, with an ego that is borderline out of control. I am always struggling to find a way to communicate with him effectively because any words that come out of my mouth that are in conflict with his views frustrate him. Like The Exec, when he hears a different opinion, he thinks, "She is saying I'm wrong." His competitive male nature says, "Fight." And that is what he does. His process is to just speak over anyone in the room who has a different point of view. My challenge is to find a way to share my thoughts without causing a threat by doing so, and to say it in a sound bite because he does not hear lengthy explanations. I have found a way. Sometimes I can diffuse him with, "I completely agree, what do you think about_____?" When he sees that I am on his side and when I present a new view as a question, he does not see the communication as an attack. Presenting my thought as a question also helps me limit my answer to one sentence, so it helps his linear listening style. What a gift it would be to be able to speak in a sound bite at will! It is really hard for me to think quickly enough to do this when I have something to say. I am trying hard to remember to think before I open my mouth, and because I have so much passion, I miss this opportunity more than I'd like. But the times I am able to do it, it works like a charm!

Another practical example I can share is the way I communicated with Casper. Casper was also a circular communicator, and a fairly linear listener, like me. I found it very easy to listen to him. He shared lots of detail on the way to his point, but it was always very interesting and insightful stuff, and I enjoyed his perspectives. Our personalities were definitely a great match, so we seemed "in sync" with our communication most of the time. Our biggest issue was having so much energy in a discussion that we frequently interrupted each other. I did struggle sometimes with my instinct to push his slow and methodical decision process because my thought process operates at warp speed. It was often difficult to bite my lip and fight the urge to grab his collar and shake him until he just made a decision! I was almost always able to keep it a silent struggle because I recognized that he needed to do things his way. It was critical that I demonstrated to us both that I was capable of giving him that respect. Of course, I only had this issue with his decision process in one area . . . his other relationships! It was important to me for any choices he made to truly be his. I always tried to remember that point to help me squelch my own desire to influence him. When I watched him struggle with his relationship situations, I tried to remember he had his own drivers behind his internal tug-of-war. Whatever those were, I tried to avoid making my own judgments and to just be an honest friend. That's why it was easy for him to convince me he that was confused for such a long time. Honestly, I could look into his eyes and just feel so much of the struggle and the emotional energy. That is what it's like to have communication beyond a surface level. I hope someday Casper realizes that recognizing you need things from a relationship that your current partner is not capable of delivering does not make you a bad person. However, lying to everyone to avoid dealing with your situation is a big negative! Casper has to reach his own conclusions all by himself. I did feel we had some very deep and meaningful discussions about relationships. I attempted to speak in his language, and tried to use my understanding of what was important to him to help me communicate well. Regardless of the outcome of my romantic relationship with Casper, I was able to communicate more effectively than I had in my previous relationships. And it was because our communication process appeared to be so strong that I felt he would get past his habit of lying. I was wrong!

So from this lesson, remember that building strong communication is fundamental to creating the type of bond that lasts indefinitely. You must understand yourself as well as your partner to be able to communicate effectively. You must communicate verbally, emotionally, and physically to truly become intimate partners. Remember that you will both likely have different communications styles, and you will have to be flexible to find a method that works for you as a couple. Focus on those things that are important to your partner as you try to craft your common language for communication. I think next time I put my chick perspective in a book, it might be solely on the topic of communication. Mastering the art of successful "guy/girl talk 101" is certainly a novel in itself!

Chapter 8

Lesson Number Seven

*"Love **DOESN'T** Conquer All!"*

Darn those fairy tales and their blasted happy endings! Why do all our childhood stories, the movies we watch, the music we listen to, almost every vision of a relationship we take in showcase a perspective that says despite any obstacle, love will undoubtedly conquer all? People, I'm sorry, it's just not the case. Unfortunately, love does *not* conquer all. I hated learning this lesson, and I still want my fairy tale! But folks, I have to tell you that having those great feelings, being wrapped up in the emotion of love, is just not enough to make your relationship work. Ok girls, I know this sounds like pure blasphemy to many of you. Sure, it feels great to be in love, there is nothing like it. But there are many practical aspects necessary for having a successful relationship, and those amazing feelings will not deliver on the practical facets of making a relationship work. Relationships don't come to a screeching halt because the feelings didn't work. They are brought down because the practical things that are missing wreak their havoc on those precious feelings until they go numb. The Beatles were wrong . . . love isn't all you need.

When I look at the high divorce rate in our country and the

number of people who seem to jump into marriage quickly, I have to wonder what impact this "love will conquer anything" preconditioning is having on each of us. Don't misunderstand my concern here. I'm not telling you love doesn't matter and relationships should just be practical. Love should absolutely be your driver! I can think of nothing more boring than a nice practical relationship with no punch! And hey, the absolute best reason to try and work out a relationship with problems is because you sincerely love each other. But I've grown to believe that you cannot allow love to blind you to other things that are important because those other things will end up haunting you later in your relationship. Great feelings do not mean you can communicate well. Great feelings do not mean you share common values. Great feelings do not mean you desire the same kinds of things from life. Great feelings do not make you compatible roommates. Great feelings do not mean you share common financial perspectives. Great feelings do not mean you enjoy the same kinds of activities. Great feelings do not even mean you will be sexually compatible. And without all these practical aspects, those great feelings are not going to survive.

As I look back on my past relationships, I can say with every confidence that those great feelings of love were there *every* time. But my relationships crashed anyway. Just look at my fallout with The Exec. I was completely in love with him, and I just knew that his love for me would motivate him to come back. I wasted a full year of my life because I stayed stuck in my fantasy that love was going to conquer all. In fact, for him, having such strong feelings was something he perceived to be a problem. He didn't like being in love because it made him unable to control his emotions. He told me that point blank during our split. But despite the fact that he was divorcing me, I was convinced his love was going to be our saving grace. It was just brutally hard for me to accept that he might have loved me but other things were so much more important to him they could cause him to leave. Could there actually be something more important than love? I couldn't even fathom the thought. But here I was, forced to consider the possibility that despite the fact that a relationship can't last without love, maybe other things also have to be present to make it work long term. Amazingly, I didn't learn this when my earlier relationships ended. How could I have ended two huge relationships without recognizing that love doesn't conquer all? After all, I ended my relationship with My Cowboy for practical reasons, and my feelings of love for Mr. Porsche disappeared because I was missing very important practical things. Nope, it took me hanging onto the fairy tale dream through twelve months of a tortuous divorce only to have it shattered in my face for me to learn this lesson. Pain is certainly a good teacher!

When I was trying to understand why I was perceived to be a high maintenance woman, I did quite a bit of soul searching. I really took a hard look at myself and what I'm all about. As I said before, this was a really eye opening process for me. There were things I saw that I wanted to do differently, and some of those things I tackled very quickly. I needed to stop being judgmental and recognize that my way isn't the only right way. I needed to be less selfish and recognize that life wasn't just all about me . . . what other people want is just as important to them as my desires are to me. But when I started to look at who I am, it became clear to me that there are things I don't ever want to change. I enjoy my independence and will always push myself hard to achieve my goals. I will always have great bandwidth, tremendous energy, and a drive to live life to its fullest potential. I am a rapid decision maker and I will continue to chase my dreams fearlessly. I must find someone who feels comfortable with these things because they are core to my personality. No matter how deep my next partner's feelings are for me, if he cannot accept these things about me, those feelings will not be enough to make our relationship work.

I also recognized that there were things that are important to me in life and in a relationship that I'm not willing to live without. I want to be with someone who believes in the concept of being partners, not in being my relationship boss. I want to be with someone who is honest, kind, hard-working, and motivated in life. I'd never make it with someone who has no drive. I want to be with someone who has a personality that is naturally a great match with mine and with someone who enjoys doing many of the same kinds of things I enjoy. I want to be with someone who will laugh with me and who enjoys conversing with me. Guess that rules out the strong silent ones! For me, these are just a few of those necessary practical aspects for a relationship. I think my "deal breakers" would be drugs, emotional or physical abuse, prejudice, and lack of motivation and energy. In the long run, if the important things I need are absent, no feelings can miraculously make a relationship work for me.

Some of you might ask how it is even possible to fall for someone who doesn't demonstrate the things that are important to you. Why would you be attracted to someone who didn't possess the right qualities? Those of you asking this question will get a detailed answer in lesson #8. There is no "why", no logic to love. It is entirely possible to experience those magical feelings before you completely understand the person you are dating. It takes time and many different experiences to get to know the practical things about a person that will indicate if your relationship can last long term. And when those feelings skyrocket, it's hard to remember to keep your feet on the ground while you look for those practical things. And many people just don't have the patience to go through this kind of process and to give the relationship time to honestly develop before they take some high-level action. Frequently the end result is jumping into marriage too soon. Perhaps we jump because we think marriage is what we are supposed to do, and we feel pressure to be "normal". Perhaps we jump because we are in a hurry to have that fairy tale. Perhaps people jump just because they need to be taken care of . . . they are not able or willing to be alone. Or maybe it's because when we have those amazing feelings, we are willing to do anything to try and make them last, and "marriage" is the step we are conditioned to take to make love last a lifetime. There are surely many reasons we rush through learning about each other and take dramatic steps we may not be ready for!

After going through this process many times now, I can tell you that I believe cohabitation to be an important step before a commitment of marriage. The reason is pretty simple. I think I need to spend time with someone every day and see what he is like in everyday situations, not just in "date" mode. It's easy to have only good times when you can retreat to your own spaces after spending a few fun hours with each other, even if you see each other frequently. I think it is also important to see how my guy will handle "less than perfect" days. It's important because every day isn't going to be perfect, and how we deal with adverse situations is going to be a huge factor in determining whether or not we can be successful long term. Those perfect days are easy to handle. But you can rest assured that your life will be filled with interesting little challenges to deal with. And how you handle those little challenges will have a huge impact on your relationship. If you take the stress of difficult situations out on each other, you can seriously drain your relationship energy. If you allow adversity to be the source of arguments, if you place blame on each other rather than tackling the issue together, if you allow the issue to control you rather than taking control of the issue, you can create enormous relationship baggage. And if you avoid dealing with issues when they are small and containable, they will only grow into big ones that will bring you down later.

My recommendation for handling life's little challenges is pretty simple... lighten up, find the humor, then tackle it head on. Laughter can be the most effective tool for dealing with stressful issues, particularly those that are out of your control. And there's always a little humor to be found. Mercy, I've managed to find twelve chapters of humor from four crumbled relationships! A positive attitude can get you through just about anything, especially when you work together to stay lifted. And if you can't find humor in your situation, just go find something else that's bound to create laughter and take a break. Rent a funny video. Go see a comedy show. Have a squirt gun fight! It's just amazing how great it feels to laugh!

But then use the humor to deal with the situation. Don't avoid it. The problems that get created when you don't address the issues frequently dwarf the size of the original issue. I realize I've already said this, but it's so important I have to repeat it. Guys, this is especially important for you, because many of you tend to think the negatives might just blow over if you just don't discuss the issue of the moment. It won't, because we girls tend to have very long and detailed memories when it comes to problems in our relationship. Things "add up" for women. The frustration women experience later is much more severe, because mentally we've linked this particular problem to several other things in our mind. And this is why you guys frequently defer to "guy talk 101", otherwise known as the half truth or dodging the question. You are concerned that if you are completely honest, you will have to handle a reaction you don't like. You are right, you probably will. But that reaction now will just pale in comparison to what you will have to deal with later! And that's where the humor comes into play . . . if you handle things with a bit of humor and keep your perspective light, the whole situation just seems less severe. It will be easier for everyone to remain composed. Girls, we must remember to appreciate the fact that if our guys are willing to do this with us, we can't punish them for failing to take the issue completely seriously. Finding the humor doesn't mean the seriousness of the situation isn't respected. It simply means we are making a conscious choice to handle things with the most positive perspective and a lighthearted approach.

I have to say that Casper and I almost always handled our bad situations fabulously . . . despite the fact that most of our bad situations were created by his lies. Even during the worst of times, we almost always managed to find the humor. I think our ability to stay light kept the tension between us at a minimum. After we would experience an initial blow up, we would send the funniest messages to each other over our two-way pagers. At one point I referred to his multiple relationships as the "love quadrangle". He turned it into a Star Trek analogy and said he was simply "lost in space, wandering in the Delta Quadrant". I reminded him that the Star Trek "Voyager" series was in its last season because even Hollywood couldn't keep audiences interested in a crew that wanders aimlessly through space forever! Our banter was always hilarious and it provided us a method to discuss our issues more calmly. When Casper and I were in Europe, I mistakenly had a travel agent book us at the wrong hotel. It was lacking simple modern conveniences . . . like a shower!! I was unsure if he was going to be angry or disappointed and had no idea how he was going to react. But rather than complain or be mean, he just found the humor. We made an adventure of it, squeezed his six foot two frame into the tiny bathtub, took photos with the owner next to the elevator "for one", and laughed the entire trip. It is one of my fondest memories and a place I confirmed that Casper and I tackle adversity with a similar lighthearted attitude.

When you travel together, you discover what it is like to be with each other constantly. There's just no place to hide! It's honestly a great indicator of what life might be like together. Talk about a great way to start uncovering all those practical little details! I definitely think travel is a great way to get to know each other very well. So for those of you who have now accepted that there might be a possibility that love doesn't conquer all, if you are looking for ways to discover those practical factors, I recommend you take a few trips, even if they are just weekend escapes. Spend as much time doing things together as you can. Give yourselves the opportunity to see each other react in a wide variety of situations. Discover if you enjoy doing the same kinds of things. It is impossible to honestly know your partner without spending time together. I think when you take this approach, if you are truly in love, the feelings grow even stronger and deeper through sharing as many experiences as possible. Honestly, with the rest of your life ahead of you, some substantial time investment on the front end of your relationship is a tiny fraction of time in the scheme of things.

Once you are in a committed relationship, the challenge becomes finding ways to continue to spend time together, to do interesting things over an extended period of time. I think it is such a shame when two people who have a great love spend years of their lives at their separate jobs, dealing with the kids individually, not making time to enjoy being with each other . . . and a few years later find themselves looking at each other and asking, "What's happened?" It's so easy to grow apart if you don't make the effort to stay connected, even when you love each other very much. Think about how much you grow and change in a few years, how many more experiences you have had today than five years ago. If you weren't spending lots of time with your partner to stay connected, how do you even know what he/she is all about now? I feel so sad when I see couples who have spent their time jointly living their own separate lives, without each other as the center of focus. After the kids have grown up or it's time to retire, they can't figure out how to enjoy each other any more. It's such a shame, and no great love can survive the challenge of constant distance . . . even if the distance happens while you are right in front of one another!

As I said earlier, I have seen that with all my relationships, my four deep loves, some form of distance was a primary destructive force to the relationship every time. So one of the practical aspects I will look for in my next relationship will be a mutual commitment to spending significant time together. I've just about had it with the loneliness anyway!! With My Cowboy, by not sharing our college time when we were both growing, changing, and having some of our most formative life experiences, we just began to head down separate paths. And at some point, I no longer felt the closeness that had always been there, the high-level connection just seemed gone. I guess you could say we grew up in different directions. I hate that I look back now and feel that relationship was one that we might have been able to save if we had just known what to do. If I could have had the understanding then that I do now, I would have understood so much more about us both. There's that hindsight! I might have seen steps we could have taken to try and reconnect. But we were just too young and without enough life experiences.

My relationship with Mr. Porsche became the victim of distance despite the fact that we were right in the same house. We did very little together on a regular basis. I spent much of my free time with the drill team I was coaching, and he spent his free time doing his racing activities. Even though I participated in several of the racing events and sincerely enjoyed it, our time spent doing things together was just so minimal we just became like platonic roommates rather than intimate partners. We both worked at separate companies all day. Neither of us could really relate to the other's career. He spent most evenings working on his racing business in the garage. I spent many evenings at practice or games with the Dallas Mavericks Dancers. We were two married people living totally separate lives. While we had a lot in common during college, we had less to share once we were married. Spending so little time together created a canyon of distance there was no hope to cross later.

The Exec and I were hugely career connected. However, we stopped spending enough time together to make that an advantage. We had our entire work perspective in common, and many interesting thoughts to share with each other. But failing to make the time to share them took a major toll. He spent much of his time in Asia, where the time zone was opposite of ours here. That made it very difficult for us to even communicate when he was traveling overseas. I traveled frequently to Mexico, and it was very difficult to synchronize our customer-driven travel schedules. We both were self-admitted workaholics. I am a firm believer in two people going after their careers with a vengeance. But recognize that if you choose to sacrifice most of your available time for each other in the process, your relationship will suffer heavy casualties. Love can't conquer all when you spend all your time doing battle separately on opposite sides of the world!

And then there was Casper. Well, we certainly had a lot of reasons to be spending time apart, starting with his girlfriend and his wife! When a relationship doesn't progress to an exclusive one, it's impossible to put in the kind of time required for it to grow into something sincerely meaningful. But I also have to admit that we both used distance as a "tool" to manage through several difficult situations. He'd be the disappearing friendly ghost whenever we got too close. I'd distance myself when I became aware he was still in those other relationships. Then there was the physical distance created when I moved away for almost a year. Upon my return, I traveled constantly on business. Personally, I was not willing to sacrifice time for my own things unless we were in a committed relationship. The lies also caused their own type of distance. It was hard to feel close when there wasn't complete trust, especially towards the end. Our relationship never had a chance for success. And I'm smart enough to recognize that my own love wasn't strong enough to conquer the obstacles on this one solo!

In addition to the distance, there were other practical factors missing from each of these relationships. My Cowboy and I both wanted something different out of life at the point we split. I needed someone to be a very active part of my life. Most of the important things that were happening to me I'd had to enjoy without My Cowboy. He was unable to attend most of my performances as a Dallas Cowboys Cheerleader, although my family was always there! When I went down to graduate school, I wanted to spend some time together every day. He still wanted his "space". He was focused on enjoying his youth. I was focused on becoming an adult. The feelings couldn't save us from what we each needed. We hit a crossroad many couples experience . . . either take the relationship to the next level or bring it to conclusion.

Mr. Porsche and I were missing most of the practical aspects a solid relationship requires. For starters, our view on marriage was very different. I thought we were going to have a partnership. He thought we were building a dictatorship. We had different views on the kind of support we should give each other. We both felt it was important for me to support his racing efforts. I even learned how to "lay up" fiberglass so I could help in our garage at night. I learned everything I could about auto racing, did research to help with his business planning, attended all kinds of races with him. In college, I even rode with him in a rally race as his navigator! He did not return the support, however, with some of my key interests. In two years he came to watch my award winning drill team perform only one time. When I told him I had been invited to audition for the Dallas Mavericks NBA charter dance team, he laughed at me for thinking I'd make the squad. He was more supportive once I made the team and did come to some of my performances, although I think he was really only there to watch the games because he loved the NBA! We just had completely different interests. There were very few activities we enjoyed together. We had different financial priorities. We had different perspectives on whether or not to have a family. We just failed to really explore these kinds of topics with each other before we were married. The end result was simply a non-stop struggle.

The Exec and I were at polar opposites on the issue of money. During our divorce, I was surprised to learn that our financial perspectives were so different, since I didn't know it was even an issue during our marriage. We seemed to have a great financial process. We took our total income as our starting pot. We deducted the amounts needed for bills and for savings, and each of us had responsibilities for paying different things. Then we each had some monthly mad money to spend any way we wanted. We maintained separated checking accounts and credit cards. What I didn't realize was that he was frustrated by the "frivolous" ways I spent my mad money . . . on clothes, makeup, etc. But it was mad money . . . it was supposed to be spent on whatever we wanted! He got frustrated with me for spending it rather than saving up for big things as he did with his. Then he wanted to use his money for big purchases, like trips, cars, and home furnishings at will, which I thought shouldn't be made without discussion. To The Exec, there was very little that was more important than money. He felt

I didn't have the same value of a dollar. He was right, because to me it was always "only money".

When we started our video business, I began to get a glimpse of the difference in our money mindset. He was very hesitant to invest our money into the company and wanted to raise it completely from others. I felt it wasn't right to ask people to invest in something I wasn't helping finance as well. Once the business failed to move quickly, I wanted to kick up our investment to shoot a test commercial. He would not invest additional money. He just wanted me to quit. I couldn't imagine letting our investors down. So, I took out a loan against my car, which I owned prior to our marriage, to pay for part of the test. He allowed me to make this financial decision knowing he was leaving me, and just three days prior to telling me he wanted a divorce.

The Exec and I also had very different perspectives on our families. As you can probably tell, I am very close to my family. I talk to them frequently, enjoy spending holidays with them, and would bring everything else to a screeching halt for any family emergency. The Exec was completely distanced from his family when we met. After spending time with my family, he tried to get closer to his, even organizing a family reunion. He told me he was thankful my family spirit was contagious. However, he never quite understood the depth of my feelings. When I wanted to move close to my family due to my father's health rather than accept the overseas transfer, he couldn't deal with it. He could not imagine postponing a business opportunity for a family matter. I thought that was just so sad.

We also had a conflicting personality trait that caused quite a bit of friction. He liked to flaunt his success with everyone. I preferred to share my excitement and good fortune with only my closest friends at the right moments. I was bothered by the way he toured people through our home pointing out the "exclusiveness" of our possessions. When he was shopping for my engagement ring, he actually asked other women at work about the size of their diamonds. During our split, he purchased a Mercedes Benz 740IL and talked about it at work so much, people began to ask me how it felt to be replaced by a car. This practical little difference created escalating tension between us.

Of course, the practical aspects that were missing with Casper were certainly baseline fundamental issues for me. Let's start with honesty. Casper was telling me lies continuously. The problem was that I fell hard and fast into what I thought was the perfect relationship before I knew there were lies. So when I got hit with his engagement the first Christmas, I wanted to believe it was an isolated incident. I bought into his "confusion" because I felt I'd been there. I couldn't imagine he might really have every intention of getting married and still be seeing me. By the time it became more clear to me that the lies were extensive and that at least one other woman was involved, I was too far into the fantasy to end the relationship. At that point, I wanted to believe he was going to change because "I was worth it". But after enough pain and the passage of enough time, I realized that he wasn't trying to change the situation at all. In fact, he was doing everything possible to escalate each of his relationships, with Snow White, with Taz, and with me. When I could finally see this clearly, I knew this had grown to become a lifestyle rather than confusion. So, despite his good qualities, I believe that Casper lacks the capability to live an honest life. And that certainly makes him an unattractive potential partner in my eyes!

The second big missing practical factor in my relationship with Casper was monogamy. Obviously, he is able to be intimate with several people during the same time period. Lots of guys can do this easily. But I certainly wasn't looking for that kind of relationship. He knew that, and of course it was the reason he chose to lie in the first place. I had no interest in breaking up a happy relationship, and I certainly wasn't interested in being one of his chicks on the side. He had to convince me we had huge potential for a lasting relationship, or I'd have been out in a minute. As I said earlier, I do think he had some level of sincere feelings for me and for Taz. Sad but true, people cheat on those they care about all the time. Affairs are a frequent occurrence in our country. But I don't believe Casper ever plans to leave his wife, and I think it's true that he loves her very much despite his bad behavior. It seems Snow White is the only one who receives some unselfish behavior from him. I believe he is just not strong enough to avoid all the temptations in life. I told him I think he is like an alcoholic who may have some sincere desire to quit drinking, but tries to quit while he's still running his tongue around the top of the glass. It disappoints me that the damage he is doing to people he cares for is not motivating enough for him to bring it to a halt. It is obvious to me that Casper and I have such different values it would be impossible to make a relationship work. I can't even imagine being able to kiss him again without wondering where his lips had been that day!

So from this lesson, I hope you recognize that while love may be the driving force of your relationship, it must be balanced by important practical factors for the relationship to last. Love was there, deep and to my core, in every one of my relationships. The practical factors that were missing brought each relationship down. I failed to give my relationships enough time to develop before I was head over heels. And by that point, I was blind to the things that were missing. Distance took its toll in all my relationships, so at least I'll be able to keep that at the top of my mind next time. I also hope that in the future I'll be able to keep my head in the game, paying attention to those practical aspects, despite the fact that my heart will probably dive right on in as usual. My greatest challenge will be remembering to listen to my head despite what my heart says. My heart has proven to me time and time again that in a battle for love, it is unquestionably the stronger of the two. Better get my brain some weapons of mass destruction!

Chapter 9

Lesson Number Eight

"There Is No 'Y' in Love"

Why? It's the million dollar question at the end of every failed relationship. Why doesn't he love me anymore? Why did she have an affair? Why did he leave me? Why was I used? Why didn't this last forever? Why can't I just get over this? Perhaps we ask questions like this because we are searching for something tangible we can grab to justify the pain. And certainly "why" is a great question to ask. In fact, the reason I started writing this book was to help myself answer two questions. Why did The Exec leave me? Why do I continue to fail in my important relationships? But of course, there are no clear answers to these questions. The heart just makes decisions for us sometimes. And when the heart is the driver, there is no answer to the question why. There is no logic, no reason, no analytical process to matters of the heart. There is no rational process that drives why you fall in love, and there is often no logic to why those feelings change. The heart is pure emotion, and what your heart needs to be happy is unique to you. Do you know what your heart needs to be happy?

I'm not suggesting that if you look back on your past relationships you won't find an answer to why there weren't happy endings. In fact, you probably will find some indicators if you can look back with complete honesty. Be prepared to recognize that you might see things you should do differently in your future. Scrutinize your own actions just as hard as the actions of the one who left you. As you've seen, I've learned a great deal by reflecting back on my past. But inevitably you will find questions that seem to have no answers. The heart does not choose a partner because it makes logical sense, the heart chooses because something makes it feel good. The heart hangs on when it shouldn't because it remembers that good feeling even when your mind sees the logical reasons you should let go. And sometimes the heart doesn't feel good anymore and lets go all by itself, despite a mind that might find many logical reasons to stay. What a complex little mess the heart can create. Why?

When I look back at my past relationships, I see a pattern. Once I find someone I think might be a good match, I go into the relationship holding my heart out on a silver platter. My heart goes first, then my mind follows. Feelings drive me completely in a relationship. I'm never looking at what's logical, what's practical, or what's healthy . . . only what feels right. Maybe that is why I am capable of a very deep love, and very stupid decisions! I hold nothing back and there is no fear for me. And isn't that a surprise, having been through the experiences I have been through? But honestly, I don't know how to do it any other way. I have no clue how to guard my emotions, or how to control them. I can certainly manage how I react to things, but I can't control the feelings. I don't say things like, "I love you," unless I feel them. I could never say things just to get a reaction from someone, or to drive behavior. Heck, I can't even be that calculating in a business meeting, I sure can't pull it off in a relationship! When I look back at the men in my life, I now find myself wondering how many of all those great lines I believed were exactly that. . . . just lines. I know that the most honest relationship I had in my life was with My Cowboy. We were so completely open with each other that it probably spoiled me. Our communication process was such a core strength. It seemed so natural. I guess I thought my future relationships would always be like that, full of trust and open honesty. The fact that I can still have somewhat of a naïve attitude towards men is amazing. But I know I will always have a tough time when someone shares with me sweet words my heart wants to hear. Go ahead, call me a hopeless romantic. I just hope next time I also remember that actions speak louder than words.

Mr. Porsche and I had really poor communication from the start of the relationship. Since that was the strength for My Cowboy and me, you'd think this would have been a big red flag for me with that relationship. But like I said, there is no "why" when it comes to the heart. Mr. Porsche made me laugh. We did things that were fun, so I gave him my heart. And then we spent no time together. He wanted me to be something that I wasn't, and whatever level of relationship we had began to disappear. It took a lot, but my heart finally disengaged from that relationship after feeling ignored for such a long time. My first clue that it was time to get out was when I slipped into a brief affair. He was someone I'd been friends with for quite a while. I ended it after only a few weeks. I knew almost immediately the affair was absolutely the wrong move for me. But I also recognized that if my relationship had been solid with Mr. Porsche, this would not have been something I would have allowed to happen. I believe people have affairs to fill things that are missing in their relationships. For me, that affair was filling the void of feeling loved. You should never stay in a relationship that makes you hurt more than you feel happy. I think my relationship with Mr. Porsche is the only one where my heart left before my mind gave up. Usually my head is saying, "You know better than this," while my heart says, "Hang in there Cinderella!" But with Mr. Porsche, it was my mind trying to convince me I needed to make my marriage work at all cost, that I was a bad person if I left my husband. I put myself through such mental anguish. My mind thought of many reasons I should stay, but my heart could not feel one. Oh what an ugly battle when the heart and the head disagree!

The Exec was able to capture my heart because it was available. He used everything in his power. He said all the right things to me and romanced me to the point of no return. To this day I still do not know if it was sincere or if it was all just part of what he thought he had to do to win my love. He said some things when he left me that indicated it was all part of a master plan. Since all that romantic behavior ended when we got married, sometimes I wonder. But I also know most couples behave differently when they are married. And that behavior change hurts many relationships. Why do we treat each other differently when we marry? Why do we allow our primary relationship to take less priority? Why? As I pointed out with lesson #5, I am committed to at least keeping all those amazing physical things at work for the long haul of my next relationship. I'll start with lots of flirting, an important yet simple thing to maintain. I will not allow other things to keep me from giving my relationship all the time and attention it needs. At any rate, my heart belonged to The Exec completely until the end. Being with him made me so very happy. He made my heart feel complete. Like My Cowboy, The Exec and I were very close friends. But my high maintenance factors were difficult for him to accept, and I guess he was unhappy more than he was happy. We spent so much time apart, putting less and less time into maintaining any kind of mental or physical connection. And that distance caused me to feel lonely and unhappy. I knew we could reconnect and fix our relationship, but his heart had checked out of the game. Why? I will probably never know the answer to that question. But I do know that he left because his heart told him to. And that was the right move for him, despite the pain it caused me.

Casper was a such a master of beautiful words, and I always believed the things he said to me. Of course, that was a big problem since so many of the things he said were lies. Somehow I managed to keep finding new trust in him during our romantic relationship. Why? Perhaps because I was too focused on being understanding, so I found justification for his lies. Obviously my heart was still in control, not my mind! But as I mentioned earlier, I was trying to look logically at what I thought I saw happening between us. I certainly understand what it is like to be confused. When you are confused, you don't really know what you want. And when you are confused, it is entirely possible to feel one way today and another way tomorrow. And I looked at my own experience with confusion and used it to justify his lies. Logic should have been telling me that three years is an awfully long time for someone to be confused! Casper knows exactly what to say to get the reaction he wants from a woman. Maybe he even believes the words at the moment they come out of his mouth, and maybe at that moment he's even feeling the emotions. I know many guys who tell me this kind of thing happens to them all the time... that they say things and mean them at the moment, but later find they feel differently. I'm not sure if Casper's beautiful words are driven by feelings, or something else. My gut says Casper speaks these beautiful words because he thinks they are things he "should" say, or because they need to be said to take the situation to the next level, or to get a specific reaction. Regardless, it is still difficult for me to accept the fact that I believed the same set of lies for such an extended period of time. Why did my heart keep hanging on when my head knew better?

Casper never seemed to fully allow his heart into our relationship, but I know I saw a little glimpse every now and then. He often told me that he knew he would fall completely for me if he allowed himself to. Why didn't he allow himself to? Why wasn't he capable of having feelings without shutting them down? Why? No answer to those questions, though believe me, I have searched and searched for them. Is it because he was hurt badly by his first true love? Is it because he just wanted to avoid dealing with his other relationships? Is it because he has successfully kept his emotions under control with Snow White for several years and is most comfortable with that? Was he still just afraid of losing emotional control and I'd have been too much of a risk? Didn't he know that true love is a wonderful gift? I will never be able to answer these questions. I accepted the fact that perhaps his heart found something with Snow White and/or with Taz that it never found with me. I also accepted the fact that perhaps he just really isn't capable of having feelings for anyone. Somehow, I'm sure I am better for having endured all this. But why?

It's funny, I'm not sure that men actually realize what an impact their words have on women. Ok, you're laughing, of course they do and that is partly why they say them. But I struggle to think that they would say some of those things if they recognized we frequently hang our entire "sense of self" on them. You see guys, since relationships are the core driver for most women, and you are the most important relationship we can have, there is a heightened importance on the things you say. It isn't that we intentionally try to blow little things out of proportion, your opinions just matter that much! So when I think about some of the things Casper said to me during this ordeal, it's difficult to accept that someone so nice could also be so cold and calculated, so purposely deceitful. Folks, I know by now you think he's just a snake, but I've got to tell you he's very giving to people around him all the time. I don't know a person who knows him well that doesn't like him. He's got some great qualities along with the negative ones. But he definitely does whatever it takes to get what he wants at the moment without stopping to consider the potential consequences. And I'm confident he does not recognize the damage he does. He's so focused on what he wants that he doesn't visualize the potential painful outcome. And when the explosion occurs, he withdraws and doesn't have to deal with the fallout he's created.

Guys, you protect yourselves to some degree with your ego. Oh yes, I hate to break it to you, men have an ego factor that is well documented. And that ego, that thing that makes you need to be the big strong man, it protects you to some degree from pain. In fact, upon the demise of a relationship, many men are capable of moving right on to the next without the blink of the eye and certainly without allowing deep emotional damage to themselves. Men certainly do not define themselves by the things women say to them. Remember the big three? Men define themselves by their accomplishments, usually in the form of a career. Perhaps that accomplishment driver helps them move on to their next relationship more quickly so they can fulfill their need to accomplish the next life challenge. Maybe they just use their logic to quickly analyze what happened, process it, then move forward. Or maybe they just avoid it, bury their pain, and carry that baggage into the next relationship!

It is women who typically define themselves by relationships and who have a high risk of doing horrible emotional damage to themselves when their relationships collapse. For the past five years, I have seriously questioned myself. I have searched deeply to find that thing that is wrong with me that turns men off. Fortunately, somewhere during the process, I have managed to discover again and again that I am a good person, and that I don't necessarily need to be "fixed". But I certainly have been looking for any behavior that I think could use adjustment to make me more compatible. I have experienced periods of extreme depression. There have been entire weekends that I have not been able to get out of bed. I'm certain there were moments when I needed to be taking anti-depressants. But I was too busy trying to be "tough chick" to even consider the fact that medication might help me. I'm sure both men and women who are driven by their relationships can probably relate to the kind of "worthless" feelings that have frequently haunted me. But when I realize that the person who finally falls for me will do so for no logical reason, I have to ask myself why I'm doing this. Why do I torture myself overanalyzing things that are completely out of my control? Well of course because being a control maniac is one of my high maintenance factors. And pondering things for extended periods of time helps me through the vicious passage of time, that four-letter word we'll talk about in lesson #10. And yet I still just ask myself that question over and over again, as if it is possible to find an answer . . . "why?"

I can't really pinpoint an exact reason I fell for any of the guys

I've loved in my life. Why did I choose each of them instead of someone else? Why did they each choose me? It's funny how you spend a little time with someone and things just seem to click, then boom . . . you're gone. It's almost as if they were each in the right place at the right time, and "ba-da-bing" they ended up my guy. I mean I met My Cowboy on a church trip, I ran into Mr. Porsche down at college through mutual friends, The Exec was one of hundreds of people I got to know through work, and Casper was just using the same home builder. These were totally normal encounters, so what was it that really drew me into each of these relationships, and what should I look for in my next one that I haven't seen yet? There has to be a way to balance the uncontrollable emotions with the right practical factors! And I hope I've managed to at least identify most of the important patterns with these lessons so I can avoid the same kinds of problems with my future relationships. But why couldn't I see all the things that were causing our problems until our relationships were over? Hindsight certainly yields great wisdom, if you allow yourself to learn from it.

So exactly what does my heart really need to be happy? I have thought about this a lot over the past three years. I have a very strong accomplishment driver that competes with my relationship driver. That's why I allow my career to sometimes take too much time away from my relationships. It's also why I'm very understanding of the time my guy must invest in his job. But when push comes to shove, my special relationship is still at my core. And for my heart to feel happy, I need to be giving love to someone special. I am more unhappy when I cannot give love than if I'm not receiving love, and that is the reason I stayed in my relationships even though they were falling apart. That is the fundamental reason I allow myself to be treated so badly for such extended periods of time. I need to receive less than I need to give. It's very hard for me not to have someone special in my life, because making someone else feel good makes me happy. I can shower my family and friends with attention, but somehow it's still not the same. My heart experiences a big void when I'm not in a special relationship. And I need very little in return to feel good . . . a thank you, a smile, or a hug all work for me. And I desperately miss that little warm feeling that comes from knowing a special someone cares.

My heart feels happy helping people. I remember the first time Casper and I flew together. A little old woman was in front of me and was having trouble putting away her bag. So I helped her, and he just seemed so touched by the fact that I would help a stranger without even stopping to think. What has happened in our society that makes helping people a pleasant surprise? Isn't that just a sad reflection of the times? My father is the most generous person that I know. He helps everyone. He would pick up a stranger on the side of the road and take him/her to their home if they needed a ride. He expects nothing in return for his generosity. He would sacrifice anything for his family. I am so thankful to have had an example like this in my life. And I think the reason I like Texas so much is the fact that kindness still seems to rule there. It is an openly friendly state. A friend and I were recently in Dallas on business and I remember her amazement at the number of people who stopped and helped with bags and doors for no reason other than genuine friendliness. People in Texas will ask if they can help you if you simply look confused. What has happened to unselfish kindness and love? Have we just become too cynical? Whatever the case, that southern hospitality is something I really miss!

Many of the books I have read say that men show love by doing things instead of saying things. My counselor told me that as well. In fact during one of my breakups, she asked me what little things this guy had done for me that let me know he cared . . . and I got horribly depressed because I really couldn't think of anything! It surprised and scared me how little attention I was being given. Maybe I am more like men in this regard. I am not happy unless I am doing something for someone. Cliché as it may sound, it just feels good to make people smile. I believe perhaps that is part of the reason Casper could not leave Snow White and just married her. She needs him completely. He does everything for her, they spend every spare minute together, and I know it makes him feel good that he does so much for her. Maybe that is why I found him so attractive, he seems to think of her first and himself last. To most guys, I guess I appear to need nothing, so maybe they feel like I cannot be loved. Maybe I haven't been very good at letting my guys love me because I'm so busy taking care of myself. Maybe I've just picked the wrong guys! But I do want someone to take care of me and let me lean on him. I do want to let someone give me unselfish love. I've been on my own so long, maybe it's just such a habit to take care of myself. I want someone who goes weak at the knees when he's with me, just like Rhett Butler did with Scarlett. She was always his weak spot. But why is this so hard for you guys to do? Guys, why does it bother you when your feelings are out of control? Is it because you have to put yourself at complete emotional risk? Is it because most of you were raised to be a tough guy, and going mushy over a sweetheart makes you weak? Why?

It's hard for me to feel like I have given so much to the men in my life and have still seen the fall of every one of my intimate relationships. And I also wonder if my guys even felt all that love I thought I was giving. Maybe there is something about the way I give love that makes it hard for guys to receive. Honestly, I cannot figure it out. So many times when I do things for people they seem to spend a ton of time trying to figure out what I was trying to accomplish, what my motives were. In fact, I think Casper spent a lot of time trying to figure out what reaction I was trying to gain. Maybe that was part of the intrigue for him, analyzing my motives. Why do guys have a hard time just accepting my love for what it is? Why is it hard to receive unselfish caring? Why?

Like I said, I ask these questions over and over, but I will never be able to uncover answers. There is no why, no reason, no logic in love. I don't think My Cowboy, Mr. Porsche, The Exec, or Casper would even be able to answer my questions. These are not things any of us really understand. But I do know that I have to accept the fact that there will always be things about my relationships that I don't understand. It is very difficult for me to handle this because I am a control maniac, and I hate to simply accept outcomes without having any influence. It is hard, it hurts, I don't want this loneliness to continue to be an ongoing situation I have to live with indefinitely. I want the fairy tale, just like all the rest of you. But I've reached a point in my life where I now understand that the fairy tale is not a guarantee. In fact, honest deep love is the exception, not the rule. If you have it, I hope you realize how lucky you are. It's a rare and precious gift, so treat it with great respect. If you don't, I hope you will hold out until you find it.

So from this chapter I hope you will learn that there will unfortunately be questions in love that are left unanswered. Feelings just defy logic, and as you can see I know exactly how hard it is accept this fact. You can try to look for the drivers behind the behavior, because actions help make those feelings happen. Those drivers might help you understand what transpired to create the current situation, just like I can recognize that my high maintenance factors had an impact on my second marriage. But when the heart is in control, there is no clear answer to the question why. And it is tough to endure the endings of relationships without answers. It is hard to accept the hurt without something tangible to blame. It is miserable to be willing to change anything to make the relationship work again, but not to know what to tackle to make it happen. And it's hard to accept the fact that you can't be sure about the things going through someone else's mind. Actually, there is a very simple answer to my biggest question . . . why doesn't "he" want to be with me? Because feelings are not logical, and this is just how "he" feels. I'm staying focused on the fact that I want to be with a man who falls for me just as hard as I fall for him. I guess somehow I've managed to fall for men who have been unavailable in some way. I have finally recognized that it is important for me to find someone who wants to be a big and PRESENT part of my life! I'm going to remember that there is no why in love and have faith that some day, when I least expect it, the right guy will walk into my life. And hey, if I'm really lucky, maybe it will be Benjamin Bratt!!!

Chapter 10

Lesson Number Nine

*Breaking Up is **HARD** To Do!*

It doesn't really matter if you are the initiator of the ending or the unfortunate recipient of the news that "it's over". Breaking up is about as close to hell on earth as you can come. Ending a caring relationship, especially a long-term one, is indeed a unique form of torture. From the heavy feelings of guilt and feeling like a "bad" person when you've decided things must end to the excruciating pain and loss felt when the stake is shoved through your heart, breaking up forces some of the most intensely unpleasant emotions imaginable. I've experienced four lengthy trips to the torture chamber, twice as the victim and twice as the executioner! Wow, how special, I'm a torment guru! Since I've actually lived both sides of this misery, my perspective in this area is uniquely balanced. I have to say that experiencing my four huge breakups has made me so much more conscious of all the little nuances that happen during the process of a split.

I've often explained heartbreak like a scene from the movie "Indiana Jones and the Temple of Doom". Picture defenseless little me standing in front of the evil man as he plunges his fist right into my chest and rips out my heart. Then he holds it up before my very eyes as it pumps its last few beats while he squeezes it into pieces before I collapse, completely destroyed. For those of you who have been so lucky that you've never had to experience a broken heart, I can only say to you, "Yes, it absolutely feels *THIS* dramatic!"

Let me share a few more details about each of my painful endings. Then I'll share some things that might be helpful if you find yourself in the dungeon of misery. When I was ending the relationship with My Cowboy, I was clueless to the dynamics that were going on. In fact, I can't remember much at all about the actual discussion when I told him I thought we should end it. I just remember the pain he went through for months afterward. I guess I had not really expected that. After all, we had not spent much time together and weren't getting along well. I was so numb. I was naïve enough to think that it was somewhat a mutual decision. The thing that really sticks out in my mind, however, is that I actually had to be fairly hard and cold for him to start grasping I was really going to end our relationship. There is no doubt in my mind that I could have handled our split much better than I did. It was so hard for me to even talk to him. I remember that when I heard so much pain in his voice, I felt so guilty that I'd been the cause that I just wanted to get away. My feelings for him were so numb that, despite the horrible guilt, I couldn't find enough love to be motivated to continue the relationship. I had checked out and was ready to move on with my life. I just wanted it to be over, and I felt even more guilt for not wanting to find a way to hang in there. I had no desire to continue any type of friendship with My Cowboy because it was just too painful to be around him.

Ending my marriage with Mr. Porsche was also horribly difficult. My mental struggle was very complicated. Despite the fact that I was very unhappy, I couldn't get past the feeling that I was a bad person for wanting to leave my husband. I felt like a quitter, and for my personality, that was also difficult for me to handle. I remember the night I finally left our house for the first time. It was Valentine's Day 1990 and we had evening plans for which he was several hours late. The frustration had grown and grown all night as I sat waiting for him to come home. It was so intense, I can't really explain it. I was so tired of feeling like I was the least important thing in his life. When he finally arrived, he'd brought me a gift from Victoria's Secret. At that moment, I was furious that he actually thought I would be interested in sex after he'd paid no attention to me for several months. I threw the nightgown at him and walked right out the door. My best friend let me stay at her house. Mr. Porsche followed me around a few nights to see what I was doing and make sure I went to her house. He begged me to come home. He even approached my parents and asked for their help. I lasted only ten days before I moved back home with him.

We began to see a counselor. I needed some impartial person to render a judgment on this relationship. Was it fixable? My hope was that she would see it was not and give me permission to leave him, but I didn't want to tell her that was what I wanted. She was going to have to discover that our relationship was beyond repair all by herself if I was going to believe it. Besides, I needed to feel like I'd taken every imaginable step to save my marriage. I wasn't going to be able to walk away without knowing that I had tried *everything* humanly possible. I thought our first few sessions were somewhat unproductive. I wasn't sure what to tell her to allow her to determine on her own if this relationship was repairable or not. Both of us were hesitant to share details about our marriage. So she just had to ask lots of questions and proved to be helpful in at least getting us to discuss some of our feelings. She helped both of us recognize that a major source of our frustrations came from Mr. Porsche's failed attempts to control me. But for me, the most profound session came on a day that he missed our appointment and I saw her alone. We had a much more relaxed conversation, and she told me that from the discussion it was very clear to her that I wanted out. She pointed out that whenever Mr. Porsche was in the room with me, I was very "wishy washy" in my statements. Even though I thought I had been very clear, she helped me see that I was lessening the severity of my true feelings because I was trying to be nice. It was after this discussion that I was finally strong enough to tell him I wanted to separate for real and found an apartment.

For a while, it was a pretty peaceful separation. Mr. Porsche and I tried to spend some time together each week trying to determine if there was still enough there to put our relationship back together. At one point, he suggested that we start a family. I remember thinking that was a pretty bad plan given the circumstances. But since he had such a traditional view of marriage and really wanted me home taking care of him, it made sense to me that he would make that kind of suggestion. I recognized that we both really wanted different things from marriage. I felt we should both have the kind of marriage we wanted, and that meant that either one of us was going to morph into a different human, or we were going to each need to find a person with the same perspective. I began the divorce paperwork. I felt really bad that I was ending our marriage. Mr. Porsche was a very sweet person, and I knew it wasn't what he wanted.

And then things started to get really ugly. Great people can behave so badly when they are feeling desperate and are in terrible pain. He got totally vicious as we began a battle over "stuff". He hired a monstrous attorney. The game was all about inflicting enough torture that I'd give up and give him all the stuff. His attorney was willing to try anything possible. He sent subpoenas to the senior executives from my office to come testify about my "mental stability". He even tried to get one of our general managers, whom I did not even know well, just because he was the top person. Fortunately, that GM was traveling, and the subpoena could not be delivered. It was horribly embarrassing for me to have to sit outside a courtroom with my senior management waiting to testify on my behalf in a stupid divorce case. This was just one of the many pressure tactics used, and the details of the many other ugly things aren't really important. But I finally got so frustrated with both our attorneys that during our depositions, I kicked them all out of the room. I told Mr. Porsche that it was ridiculous that we were allowing strangers to encourage us to be nasty to each other, and it was costing us both more money to fight than to just settle things ourselves. So we drafted our own agreement right there. Sometimes attorneys are great, but often they are so focused on developing a strategy to crush the other party that they make the worst of an already bad situation. At least we were able to bring our relationship to closure on our own terms and to part peacefully. We didn't maintain contact, but we were both able to move on with our lives wishing good things for each other.

You already have many of the details of the split from The Exec. I went into complete shock the night he told me he wanted a divorce. Those words coming out of his mouth hit me like a grenade. But then the initial pain quickly turned into feeling completely dazed and confused. All I could think about was finding out why he wanted a divorce so I could fix it. Something inside just kept telling me not to worry, as soon as I understood, it would all be ok. Somehow I was expecting some magic information that would provide me with the solution. And I wanted to find that information at that exact minute. I was hysterical. I was crying uncontrollably and was yelling at him. I begged him to explain to me why we couldn't at least try to save our marriage. He realized that I wasn't just going to agree to the divorce, and that was why he ended up telling me that if I wanted any chance for a future, I had to agree to get a divorce at that time. He told me that perhaps we could indeed make a fresh start if we completely ended the relationship in its current form. He told me that if I loved him, I would do this for him because it was really important, and he needed to see that I could give up control. What was I going to say to that? Please don't ever use love as such a weapon. It was horribly painful to feel I had to go through a divorce to prove my love, but I was willing to do it. As you know, I spent the next eleven months trying to find any way to bring us back together, to get that fresh start. His talk of potential was nothing more than false hope for me to cling to. And cling I did for an extended period of time. The actual paperwork was not a big deal. I didn't care if I took anything from that marriage. He wanted all our stuff, and I was determined not to have another battle over material things. We did split most of our furniture, but he took all our financial assets, and I took all the debt from our failed business. I'm still paying off the debt from that marriage! I did want to part that relationship as friends, and we did make an attempt to continue to communicate. But for me, it was too painful to get along with someone I'd been so close to, yet not be able to have the romantic relationship. I just found I didn't want him to be an active part of my life anymore. He'd ripped my heart out, and hearing his voice was a constant reminder of the pain. So that was that.

There were so many blow-ups with Casper, and each episode was a step toward the final ending. There was never a full blown relationship, so there was never a "hey this isn't going to work for me" kind of discussion. Each time I discovered the lies, I'd be out of the relationship for weeks, sometimes months. But the last time, he'd been blatantly telling me for several months his relationship with Taz was completely over. He had told me she'd decided that he was never leaving Snow White and that she had given him a deadline. He told me that when he failed to meet it, she walked away. I absolutely believed that at some point, Taz was probably going to get that strong. Any time I questioned his "unavailability" during those few months, he'd try and make me feel bad for questioning him. So when I found out this was a complete fabrication and Taz had never left his side, I was so angry I'm sure smoke blew right out of my nostrils! I don't recall being that mad at any other moment in my entire life. I felt used, violated, and manipulated. But mostly, I felt stupid. I was just as angry with myself as I was with Casper because I had seen the signs and had ignored them. My gut had alerted me, and my gut had been right! I had walked away from the deal so many times and had sworn not to be sucked in again unless I could verify that Snow White was out of his house and Taz was out of his life. I couldn't believe that not only had he lied at that level, but that he made me cry because I questioned my trust for him. Casper, Taz, and I had a screaming fit on the phone after Taz and I discovered he was still sleeping with us both. I wrote him a letter telling him how I felt, and he paged me to tell me he was sorry. I told him I'd have to do some healing and get stronger before I could even speak to him. It was over a month before I could even speak to him on the phone. During that period, I did some really hard thinking. Despite the fact that I didn't agree with the things he'd done and that I was extremely hurt by his actions, I did still see some good qualities. I had no "in love" feelings anymore. But I did feel a fondness for the friendship, almost like you feel when a family member does something bad, but you still care for that person. I decided I would try to forgive him, and that has taken lots of work. Sometimes I still feel very hurt, but I found myself more at peace after I forgave him and let go of all the anger. I also forgave myself for being blinded by love. So Casper and I finally talked, and decided to try and keep our friendship intact. I think the reason we are able to still be friends is pretty simple. Our personality match was real and our friendship was there long before anything else. We both went into the romance knowing he had some big obstacles to clear for us to be together. While I never imagined he'd be lying like he did, I did recognize early that there was a risk he might not be able to end his relationship with Snow White. We can never go backwards and erase all the bad things that have happened. But we can make a conscious decision to go forward differently, and that's exactly what we've done. Casper is the first person I've managed to maintain some level of friendship with after the romance was gone. And it has been a great thing to find a positive place for Casper and me to function after all the things that have transpired.

So, twice I was the executioner delivering the fatal blow. Once I was the victim watching my heart be ripped from my body. And once I spent years in the dungeon being tortured until I took a blow powerful enough to break my chains so I could walk out a free woman. And despite all the pain, I'm a better person for having lived to tell about it! What did I take away from all these breakups that can possibly help you? I learned plenty of things that might help you end your relationship gracefully whether you are on the trip to the guillotine or the one dropping the blade.

As the executioner, my overriding rule for you is be merciful. Think clean, quick, painless death. You probably went through a lengthy and difficult decision process to make the decision to end your relationship. Then you probably agonized many more hours trying to plan the perfect setting and trying to come up with the perfect words. I'll bet there were several moments when you attempted to have your hanging ceremony, but you just couldn't get the fatal words out of your mouth. Let me start by helping you recognize that the perfect moment will never come. There is no good time to break someone's heart. The more time you allow to pass, the more memories you build together, the more experiences that transpire between you, the more difficult it will be to break up. I actually know several guys who ticked off YEARS staying in their relationships because they couldn't actually deliver the ending. In fact, a few of them actually moved away just because they couldn't find a way to break up with their girlfriends. I've always been astonished by this fact. Folks, it doesn't get any easier for either of you if you wait. I wish I could tell you that there is something you could do, some step that will make it easier, but there isn't. It's just gonna suck, so set your expectations appropriately.

If you can finally utter the words, "It's over," be prepared for an extremely emotional reaction. It's critically important that no matter what kind of reaction you get that you stand your ground and send a consistent "it's over" message. The most kindhearted thing you can do is avoid dragging your partner up and down through the yo-yo of indecision and false hope, even during the initial discussion. I promise, having lived both sides, the moment your victim is going to begin the healing process is the moment he/she can grasp that there is no hope for resurrection. Again, quick, clean death! One fatal blow is much easier than being tortured over an extended period of time going through, "It's over. It's gonna work out. It's over. It's gonna work out . . ." You might think you are being kind trying to prepare your victim for the end, trying to soften the blow. You're not. Sharp blade, take the head off with one whack, don't chop away painfully over time. You will feel horribly guilty. You will feel like a mean cold hearted person. You will be confused and ask yourself over and over if you've done the right thing. You will be convinced that no other human on the planet is as awful as you. These feelings are all normal, so don't let them get to you. Just be sure you think through everything completely before you take any action, and if you are sure it's the best decision for you, execute and don't look back. If the things that cause you to want to end your relationship are just behaviors, those are things that can be changed. You might want to have a serious, "I'm going to have to leave if these things don't change" chat rather than an "I'm done" session. But if you see core differences, the kinds of things you know are core to the personality of your partner, please recognize you will have to make a decision to live with those issues or get out.

When you tell your victim it's over, you are going to have the urge to justify your decision. It's fine to share your reasoning. Your victim is going to need the information. But please be realistic. There is absolutely nothing you will be able to say that will cause your victim to respond with, "Of course, I understand completely. You are right, we should break up." It isn't going to happen. All your victim will want to do is stop the breakup from happening. So for each reason you detail, your victim will deliver a counter response either aimed at convincing you that you are wrong, or convincing you that he/she can change. It is going to be difficult not to give in. It is going to seem really cold, but you will have to say no to the request for another chance. If you've gone through a solid thought process on the front end, remember you are at this point for good reason. Give yourself permission to do what you have to do. You don't have to justify your actions. You don't have to prove you are "right" to take the action. But at least be merciful and chivalrous. You are the one making the decision to kill the relationship. Fall on the sword, take responsibility for being the executioner, and just say "It's what I want. I wish it wasn't, but it is." Don't spend countless hours trying to justify your decision and convince your victim that he/she made you do it.

Once you've gotten through the initial discussion, go away and let the person heal. STAY AWAY. It's very confusing to have the person who ripped out your heart checking in to see if you are ok. After all, "If you care so much about me, why did you break up with me?" It's natural to want to help your victim through his/her pain. It lessens the feelings of guilt. It feels "nicer" than being cold. You've been the one to provide support for all kinds of things for this person over some period of time. But please recognize you cannot be the one to help your victim through this, or he/she might not ever let go. Your victim will have to lean on other friends, on family, on God, on him/herself. It is impossible to let go of the person you love when they are sitting in front of you showing how much they care. Letting go of that makes no sense. So please stay away and allow the victim to begin to heal. Don't be in their face giving them fresh pain with each conversation. It's going to be hard, but you both will need the space. This doesn't mean you can never be friends again. It just means you need to allow enough healing to transpire before you try. Let your romantic relationship have a peaceful death before you try to build a different type of relationship with the victim. Allow him/her to grieve the loss. Allow yourself to grieve the loss. Be merciful.

Ok, now let me share some things for all you victims out there. You will feel shocked, angry, depressed, confused, grief stricken, and probably many other things. You are probably going to have a traumatic reaction. You may do some stupid things, either out of revenge or in an attempt to salvage the relationship. Remember me sitting outside The Exec's house calling every fifteen minutes until the other girl left? Remember me writing letters, taking him on trips, doing anything possible to make him interested in saving the relationship? Remember lesson #7, love doesn't conquer all? If your partner wants out, please recognize that it is probably the best decision for him/her. I know it's really hard and not what you want to hear. But you deserve to be with someone that really wants to be with you, yes? So try to keep yourself from taking all those desperate actions in an attempt to bring your partner back because it's even more painful when they fail to work. And try not to lash out with revenge. Remember me throwing water on Casper? Just remember that losing you is going to be a crushing blow to the executioner as well, even though you won't see it at the time. Fight the urges you will have to call the executioner and talk about it. I know you will be looking for that piece of information, that "ah ha" that could help you turn things around. But please recognize that no discussion will give you that information right now. It's going to be a really long time before you will be able to look back and understand, if you ever can understand. You will be feeling all that love, and you will wonder why someone who loves you wants to leave. It won't seem possible, but it is. Remember again that it takes more than love to make a relationship work. There is just no why in love.

I'm going to spend the next chapter explaining lots of ways to deal with your pain, so I won't do that now. But the best thing you can do for yourself is recognize that there is probably a better relationship out there for you. I know it's difficult to see that while you are in pain. But focus on the fact that you are now free to go find it. Focus forwards and think about your future. Don't lie in bed thinking about all the things you miss. Try not to let yourself feel worthless and defective. I know . . . it's hard to feel good about yourself when the person you love leaves you. Let yourself heal a bit before you try to spend all those hours analyzing what went wrong. Remember that it's natural to have all the horrible feelings you are experiencing, and just take comfort in the fact that you are going to feel better at some point. It's just going to take a while. This is out of your control, and you can't fix it. Let go. Be thankful for the positive things you had in this last relationship, and know that after some time passes, you will be ready for something even better. I promise. I know you think you will never find something as good as this thing you just lost. I felt that way every time one of my relationships crashed. But guess what . . . each of my relationships was even better than the one before. I've been able to handle the ending with Casper so much better than my earlier ones. The hardest part with Casper wasn't actually the end, it was spending all those months in the torture chamber! I'm confident my next relationship is going to be the most fabulous! Look at all the wonderful things I've learned through my experiences, and how much better equipped I am for my next relationship. I'm so much more in tune with what I need to look for in a person to be successful. Hopefully, you now have a few new tools to use next time too!

Folks, it's because I've been through all this so many times that I recognize breakups are not just cut and dried. It's the fundamental reason I bought into Casper's confusion for such a long time, and it's why I can still say I think he had some sincere feelings. It really is that hard to end a long-term relationship. It is really difficult to make a decision to let go of something that plays such a major role in your life. What if the next one isn't as good as what you have now? What if you never find someone else at all? No one wants to be alone. It's really hard. Trust me, I've spent most of the last five years by myself, and I know exactly how hard and scary it is. Heck, I've spent most of my adult life by myself despite my relationships! I know it's really tempting to hang on to that "not so hot" relationship until a better one comes along. But don't do that. Don't hang onto a relationship that isn't working. It is so unfair to the other person. You are wasting time both of you could be spending in a much happier relationship. Don't cheat yourself, and don't cheat your partner. If you want something different, be brave enough to let your partner move on and find someone they can make blissfully happy. Don't you think he/she deserves that? How are you really going to find a better relationship until you let go of this one? You won't have enough time to spend with your new potential love to really see if it works. And if you are already in a relationship and meet someone new, that person might have concerns about your ability to be faithful. What kind of message does it send when you have a girlfriend or a husband at home and say yes to spending time with another person? Hey, I'm not saying it will never happen to you. I started dating The Exec during my separation from Mr. Porsche and before I knew what I really wanted. And look at what I went through with Casper. It's very rarely so clean and simple. All I'm suggesting is that you be brave enough to end your relationship if you already know that it isn't going to work for you long term. The ending will only be much harder to do later, really.

I am sincerely amazed by the number of people I know who have to be in a relationship, even a lousy one. I can count on one hand the people I know that have lived for a time by themselves. I know many girls who have never even been without a boyfriend for five minutes, who have never done the most basic things like pay a bill. Their fathers took care of them until their boyfriends took over. Some of these girls have never made a decision on their own. I know it's much easier to have someone to spend time with. And girls, I know sometimes it's easier to have someone take care of you. I can't stand eating dinner by myself, not having anyone help me move my heavy things in my house, not having anyone special with whom I can share my really exciting news or my hard days. One of my hardest days on my own was shortly after my first divorce. I was trying to open a jar of pickles, and was not strong enough to loosen the lid. I sat on my floor and cried because I had no one to help me with my pickles. And then I got mad ... so I got creative! I used my rubber gloves to grip the lid, and "pop" those pickles were open! It was a very empowering moment for me. My last real vacation was in 1996 because I can't imagine going to some exotic cool place all alone. I've mastered doing movies by myself, but haven't been able to tackle those vacations. And most of my girlfriends are married or have boyfriends, so I don't have a pool of gals I can drag along with me! It's the pits to be alone. And guys, I recognize that many of you need to find a way to enjoy sex on a regular basis, and that it's much easier to find one compatible person for this than to keep sorting through strangers. That gets old pretty fast, especially once you get a little more mature! But I have to tell you, spending some time on your own is a really good thing. It really helps you develop a clear sense of who you are and what's important to you. It allows you to be very focused on accomplishing things that are important to you. And when you feel good on your own, I believe you actually have more to give to someone else. I think spending some time on your own lets you grow into yourself as a person.

So, from this chapter, I hope you have had an opportunity to catch a glimpse of what it's like to be the executioner, and what it's like to be the victim. I hope if you take your partner to the Temple of Pain, you will be a most merciful executioner. Don't torture your victim and leave him/her in the dungeon of misery for extended periods of time. And I hope if you have to be the victim, you will able to endure the relationship death a bit more calmly. I hope each of you will take the time during your breakup to recognize what the other person is probably dealing with. It's an extremely difficult ordeal no matter which side of the fence you are on. Try to be kind and understanding to each other, despite whatever heated emotions you are experiencing. Some day you will be able to look back and feel better because you handled things well. Don't fear spending some time alone. Getting to know yourself is not so bad, and you will emerge a better person having gone through the process. If you are not happy in your current relationship, take some kind of action. Life is too short to cheat yourself or your partner from total happiness!

Chapter 11

Lesson Number Ten

"Time is a **4**-Letter Word"

If there is any cliché I HATE with a passion, it is the phrase, "Just give it time." Time should be right up there with the rest of those ugly four-letter words! Unfortunately, time is absolutely what it takes to heal pain. (Pain, also a four-letter word!) I now consider myself an expert in the area of pain management. In the past five years of my life, I have endured my second divorce, the failure of a business dream, the sudden deaths of some close friends, and the realization that the man I thought was my soul mate was a master of deception, just to name a few. What I would pay for one day that was not twenty-four more hours in a character building period of my life! This year marks my fifth set of holidays on my own. Holidays are really hard for me to handle. I now understand why there are more suicides during the holiday season than any other time of year. And do you realize we only have two months, June and August, that are free from major holidays that are enhanced by a special someone? The pain of loneliness is horrible, I would not wish the feeling on anyone. I wish I could say that the time it takes to recover from heartbreak is like a reflective walk through a lovely park, but it's more like a journey straight to hell and back. And there are so many caverns of torment to get caught in along the way. Ugggghhhh, the agony of it all!

During my first divorce, I was frequently very depressed. I was a "failure" at marriage. "Shame on you for not finding a way to make this work," I said to myself. When I started to see The Exec before my divorce paperwork was final, I added "moral pressure" to my equation. Here I was, dating someone while I was technically still married. And because I felt so happy when I was with The Exec, my feelings of guilt were actually enhanced. I was causing Mr. Porsche, whom I loved very deeply, intense pain while I was out there feeling good. It was very hard to give myself permission to be happy, and my counselor helped me with that. One of the really important things my counselor told me was to be sure to take really good care of myself. But depression makes it really tough to take care of yourself. There were days when all I could do was lie in bed and cry. There were days when I couldn't eat anything at all. There were days when I was so on edge that I would snap at anyone who spoke to me. But the more time I spent with The Exec, the more happiness I felt. And that kept my down days to a minimum. I leaned on The Exec heavily to get through my divorce. It was a very difficult time, but I was finally able to recognize I was not a bad person just because I wanted to be happy. And I recognized that I was not a mean person because I saw that my husband couldn't provide what I needed, nor could I be the girl he was looking for. So I stayed focused on my new happiness, and the time passed very quickly.

When The Exec dumped me, I was simultaneously enduring the crash of my business. It was incredibly difficult. I had just gone back to my corporate career and our separation was very public. There are no words to describe the pain I felt. The feelings of rejection and total worthlessness. The big empty hole where my heart used to be. The constant loneliness, the humiliation of everyone knowing my life was shattered and that my husband didn't want me. The feeling that I wasn't good enough. The feeling that for the first time, I was a failure in business. The guilt from losing the money of people who had believed in me. There was so much grief to handle simultaneously. I saw my counselor again, and she asked me what I was I doing to take care of myself. At least I was fortunate to have a job I loved, dance classes with friends I enjoyed, my family and childhood friends close by since I was back in my home town. And then there was God providing me with enough divine intervention and strength to remind me I was never completely alone. I was blessed with an amazing support structure! I would not have made it through that time in my life without all those things. It was easy for me to see that there was no one, including my counselor, who could fix my sadness. It was just going to be up to me. Spending that whole year hoping The Exec was going to come back to me only increased the pain, and what a shame that I did not learn lesson #7 sooner because I made things much harder on myself waiting for love to conquer all! I think the thought that The Exec might come around was just easier than facing the fact that I was going to be alone for a while, despite the fact that I'm "little miss independence". I prolonged my pain because I could not let go. I kept myself in the dungeon for no reason. Oh well, at least I didn't turn to some other man just to save me from the loneliness! Feeling like I was a "tough chick" made me feel a little better about myself. It would have been much healthier for me to recognize that it was his loss, and that certainly would have been a faster way to deal with his departure from my life!

 The pain I experienced during my romantic relationship with Casper brings new meaning to the word torture. At times it was the deepest pain I've ever felt, but all my practice helped me deal with the situation pretty well most of the time. This pain was different. This was pain from betrayal, and in my thirty-something years, I've never before dealt with that. It's was also about the loss of my entire dream of true love, not just losing the relationship. One of the toughest things about time is that while it passes, you spend countless hours thinking about the very cause of your pain. Casper appeared to be exactly the kind of man I always dreamed about, despite the horrible circumstances. He wasn't perfect, and I was able to clearly recognize that during our relationship. But there were so many times when he did seem just perfect for me. This person that I trusted was able to look me right in the eye and craft huge lies. Most of the time, I couldn't tell. How will I know next time that I can trust the guy? I accept the fact that Casper wasn't quite the person I thought he was. But how will I be able to tell in my future if the next guy is before I am too far into the relationship to avoid the monster pain? I might have been nothing more than a toy for Casper. How will I know next time if what I think I see is real? I won't, so I'll just have to be willing to take a risk again. The feeling of complete stupidity I felt at the end of my romantic relationship with Casper was the absolute worst part for me. I really beat myself up mentally for taking so long to recognize what was going on. The depression I endured during our roller coaster affair was the worst of my life. I was primarily alone in Florida with only a few close friends. I missed that huge support structure I have at home in Texas. I was terribly lonely all the time. I spent way too much time lying in bed feeling so sad, crying until my eyes were swollen and raw. Most of the time I couldn't even find the energy to work out. And when I was in the deepest stages of my depression, I even found it difficult to stay focused at work. I had never before experienced pain that was strong enough to distract me from my job. The pain was uncontrollable. I'd be on a plane for a business trip and tears would just roll down my face. Funny, this was all happening while I was in the relationship . . . once I was out I was better! When I let it go, I started the healing process. And despite the loss I felt from letting go of the relationship, that pain was so much less than the pain of holding on!

There is no easy way to pass the time when you are heartbroken and depressed. Unfortunately, it takes time passing to help you heal. It is important to allow yourself to feel the pain, even though it will be an awful experience. Don't ignore it, or later in life you will have unbelievable baggage to deal with. When you need to cry, do it. When you need to lie in bed all day, do it. When you need to call your friends and talk about how much you hurt until they can't stand it, do it. But balance all those activities with some activity that will help you feel better. Exercise, even if you are just walking briskly around the block while you cry. You will be amazed at how much better you will feel with a little exercise. My counselor says exercise helps replenish the chemical that depression drains from your brain. Be sure to eat, even when it's hard. Try to eat some solid food, even if it's just a piece of fruit. If you can't eat something whole, have a vitamin drink. If you don't eat, you will only have less energy, and that will make you feel worse. If it's food that you crave, try to stay focused on healthy things, like fruits and veggies. If you must have ice cream, have a spoonful or two instead of the whole pint. Drink plenty of water. Remember you will need to refill all those tears! Try to focus on your job, your children, a hobby, anything you can do to help you pass a little bit of time every day. I promise that even though it feels like you can't make it through the day, you will feel better very soon. I know that it is easier to lie in bed and dwell on all the bad things in your life. But force yourself to get up and find one positive thing each day. Remember that God will be on your side the whole trip. Take baby steps. Just think of making it through the next hour or even the next five minutes, and don't worry about what's coming next month. Pain can be overwhelming. It seems as though the hurt will just never go away. But even though time feels like the enemy, I promise it will be your best friend in the long run. Time is indeed the thing that will eventually make that horrible pain go numb.

Having spent so much time in tremendous pain, I can share with you some things I found that helped me cope. While I have not yet mastered keeping myself from becoming depressed, I am able to use four simple steps to dig out very quickly. These steps are things that I do and enjoy by myself. My depression process is RP^2R: Relax, Pamper, Play, Reflect.

First, I relax. I allow myself to have all the sad feelings because

I think if I avoid dealing with them today they will be worse tomorrow. So the first thing I do to relax is have a giant "release cry". I just cry and cry until I have no more tears. I find that if I put some damp cotton balls in the freezer, I can put them on my eyes after my release cry and they won't be quite so sore. I lie on my bed in the dark with my ice-cold soft cotton and rest for a bit. I try just to breathe, and not to think. This whole process makes me totally calm. I also read to relax. I read things that entertain me rather than challenge me mentally for relaxation. I can spend hours with fashion magazines. Reading interesting biographies also helps me relax.

Next, I focus on pampering myself a little bit. My most simple pamper trick is a bubble bath. There's something about being surrounded by wonderfully aromatic little bubbles that feels quite extravagant. If I'm in need of extra-special treatment, I go have a facial. For me, nothing feels more decadent than spa time. I'd like to go to a destination spa some day and completely escape for an entire week. I'm actually saving up my hotel points and airline miles so that I can go to Maui and enjoy the spa at the Hyatt without a huge price tag. It's going to be my present to myself for surviving all this and completing my book! I might treat myself to a special dinner, I might try new makeup, or even spend time trying a new hair style. Any small thing I can do to make myself feel a little spoiled goes into my pamper category.

Then I play! My favorite play time is dance class. There is nothing for me like a great hip-hop class. It's one of the few things I do that makes it impossible to think, so my brain can actually relax. I'm so focused on following the steps, I don't have time to dwell and over-analyze other things going on in my life. And of course, I get the added benefit of the extra energy from working out. I like to go to the gym when I can't make it to dance class . . . but it's not quite the same level of fun for me. My mind can still wander all over the place while at the gym! Another form of play for me is shopping. For me, there is something amazingly peaceful about being in a mall. I love the whole process of going store to store, finding interesting new outfits, and looking at new makeup. I just enjoy everything about shopping. I never get bored while shopping, and I can spend an entire day in a mall easily. My challenge here is that when I'm depressed, I lack my usual financial discipline! When I'm sad, I tend to splurge and spend too much money . . . particularly on those darn expensive shoes! My temporary fix for this has been to focus depression shopping on small things for my pamper process. I buy new bubble bath, body scrubs, or scented candles. It's much less financially painful! I also use work as play. I get relentlessly focused on some big project. I often use my work as an escape, as a prime distraction. Again, I can keep my brain from spending too much time analyzing my pain by involving it in a business challenge. This is again a little dangerous because I'm already a workaholic. But work does give me sincere pleasure and gives me lots of energy. I think of my work as fun, which is why it's "play" for me. That is also why I cannot imagine having a job I didn't just love!!

Finally, I reflect. My pool is my favorite place of peace for reflecting. I love floating on my raft, feeling the warm sun, and listening to the waterfalls. I reflect while floating in my pool two ways. The first is through long personal talks with God. I ask God to help me deal with all the tough things. I ask God to help me understand. I always feel better when I have these little chats because I am able to see things more clearly for myself and feel comforted by the help I know I will always have. For me, God is a big source of personal strength. I don't spend much time in church, but I like my relationship with God. It's funny . . . I can throw my most personal relationship details out here for you to judge, but my relationship with God is something I consider to be so private that I struggle to put this little bit on paper! Sharing my thoughts with God is sincerely my most private personal time. The other thing I do to reflect while in my pool is listen to music. I often find lyrics that describe how I'm feeling, and it helps me recognize that I'm dealing with the same kinds of things millions of other folks are experiencing every day. Somehow it helps to know

I'm not the only one! I also enjoy just getting caught up in the beat of the music. Music provides such a great escape. Finally, when I'm not floating, I reflect by writing. Writing helps me understand why I'm having the feelings of the moment. It helps me learn what I want to do differently next time if I get things down on paper. It's almost as if my paper gives me a more objective point of view. I don't keep a journal. I only write when I feel like reflecting. It's not something I can do when I'm in the depths of depression because I don't have clarity at those moments. Writing is something I do as I'm digging out.

So there you have my RP^2R process for pain management. Relax. Pamper. Play. Reflect. While I'm sure you will find your own unique activities that cover each of these categories, I strongly recommend you try these four steps if you are having trouble letting the time pass. I also recommend that you gather for yourself a wide variety of things you can put into your "play" category. I'm adding golf and scuba to my list! I pick things that I can do alone simply because I don't have access to many folks to spend time with close by. You certainly don't need to feel the need to isolate yourself and spend too much time alone! I think it is much healthier to spend play time with people you enjoy. However, if you are in a similar situation, it's much better to go play alone rather than lie in bed feeling depressed watching television. Another thing that helps me is to go participate in a charitable activity. It's always gratifying to help someone else in trouble. I spent time on the board for a local United Way organization, have walked in relays for cancer, and have donated lots of time for kids. I find this is important to me at all times in my life, but it's particularly helpful when I'm in pain.

Now I'd like to talk to you about a dangerous trap you must be careful to avoid. Don't let the fact that your relationship has crashed and you can't stand all this pain let you become something you are not. I know it's hard to let the time pass, and it seems like "changing" so you can get back into your relationship seems like a better plan. But stay true to yourself and who you are.

It's perfectly fine to find some behaviors you'd like to improve. It's healthy to recognize that you are not perfect, and to take steps to grow and improve. It is not healthy to become something you are not just to stay in a relationship that isn't working. Why have a relationship if you have to present an imaginary version of yourself to be compatible? Maybe it seems easier to morph into whatever thing your partner wants. And maybe it is easier to do that than to have enough self-confidence to stay focused and be true to yourself. I could have saved my first marriage if I had been willing to stay home and become the doting housewife. But how miserable would I have been as a person if I had to give up all the things that made me truly happy? I almost made this mistake when The Exec left me. I was ready to become anything he wanted to stay together. I was so desperate I was ready to move to China. People, I don't want to live in China. There are places I'd enjoy as an overseas assignment, but China just isn't one of them. But I was willing to go be miserable to save my relationship. I was determined to find a way to show him I could completely give up control since it was such an issue. And now I'm wiser, and I know that I'm never going to be able to completely give up control of my life to someone else. I know that I need a relationship partner, not a relationship boss. I know many women fear the thought of having to be on their own so much that they are at great risk for turning themselves into whatever it takes to save their relationships. I know taking care of yourself can be a scary thought. My heart goes out to those of you who feel trapped by your situation, unable to be yourself for fear your partner will leave. I'm thankful for my education, and for the confidence my parents gave me. Both these tools allow me to attack life and remain in control of my own destiny. I encourage each of you to take steps to insure you can stand on your own two feet. There is nothing more empowering than having confidence in your ability to take care of yourself. Remember that pickle jar!

How is it possible to be in a long-term relationship without being yourself? When The Exec left me, he told me that he had never been himself with me. He had only presented this "person" he thought I wanted him to be. It was so hard to hear him say that. How could this person I loved so much be uncomfortable being himself with me? How could someone spend almost seven years in a relationship without being himself? I could not understand how this was possible. It's natural to want to present your best side, especially in the beginning of the relationship. But sooner or later, you must determine if the real you is compatible with your real partner. If you hide your true self, you are cheating your opportunity to discover the potential for the relationship. Isn't that what it is all about, finding a person who loves the person you actually are? Especially if you want to find a forever partner, isn't the rest of your life an awfully long time to spend being something you are not? How could he have married me if he wasn't able to be himself with me?

The Exec also told me he did not know who he really was anymore. I think he was really close to mid-life crisis and at that age where men start to ask, "What am I really doing with my life?" Have any of you guys hit that point? He was unhappy with his career direction and his career defined who he was . . . therefore everything in his life had to change. He told me that I had such a strong sense of myself he could never be with me until he understood who he honestly was. Regardless of whether or not this was true, he was correct on one issue. I do have a very strong sense of who I am and what I am all about, and I always have. That makes it difficult for me to understand how it could be possible not to know who you are, but I guess I have seen this enough to accept that it is completely possible. I recently saw the movie "Runaway Bride" with Julia Roberts and Richard Gere. She has run out of four wedding ceremonies, and he helps her realize that she doesn't really know who she is. She eats whatever kind of eggs her partner likes. She isn't pursuing her love of art as a career. She is living her life for others and not for herself. I see so many women who don't work because their husbands don't want them to. They don't have dreams of their own and don't have lives of their own. I interact with men every day who feel threatened by these kinds of things. That kind of perspective is hard for me to understand.

How can you honestly have anything to offer to your partner if you don't have your own dreams, your own pursuits? I know . . . people have relationships for many different reasons. Everyone wants something different from a relationship. Sometimes a relationship provides companionship. Sometimes it's just for sex, and sometimes it's for financial support. Sometimes it is for love and emotional support, and sometimes a combination of all these things. Do you understand why you are in your current relationship? Wouldn't the best fit be finding someone who wants the same kinds of things? Relationships require compromise, so I'm not telling you that understanding yourself and staying true to what's important to you means that you should always get your way. I'm saying that if you don't pick someone who has a core in line with yours, you will be faced with continuous life compromise on issues that are way too important to sacrifice. And the rest of your life is an awfully long time to spend it constantly giving up what is really important for you! Compromise certainly has to happen to have a successful relationship. I'm just suggesting that your personality should not be one of the things you give up. Don't be so desperate that you give up who you are!

Time causes another complication for us in life. We change over time. As we experience different situations and we enjoy new things, we grow. So even if you know what you want out of life today, how is it possible to make a relationship last when you are going to change throughout time? How do you know if the person you are happy with today will be the person who makes you happy tomorrow? You don't . . . there is no way to insure forever happiness. But if you recognize right now that you will both change over time, and you choose someone who has a "core" comprised of things that are important to you, and you both understand it takes flexibility in your relationship to have longevity in your relationship, I believe you can make it last. I've shared with you the things I believe to be my core. I have always been very independent and confident. My entire life I have had tremendous energy and a lot of bandwidth. My passion has been part of my personality since day one. Love is the most important thing to me. I would sacrifice anything for those I love. No matter how I change in my life, those things among a few others will probably be constants. My personality, my core, this will be the thing that is still with me when I'm 80 years old. My activities, interests, behaviors, and the way I reflect who I am, those may all change. So if I can find someone whose core personality complements mine naturally, and we spend lots of time doing things together so that we both grow and change from a similar set of experiences, we enhance our chance of success. Time doesn't have to force us to change so much we can't possibly remain compatible. We cause those changes ourselves by not doing the things that help us stay connected to one another.

So from this chapter, please recognize that time may seem like the enemy, but it's not. Everyone feels desperate when they are hurt. In fact I remember reading an article on breakups that reminded me Gwyenth Paltrow had just been dumped by Brad Pitt and was probably sitting at home crying just like I was right at that very moment. People survive their broken hearts even though it's incredibly hard. But the only way to heal the pain is to let the time pass and deal with it. No one can do the healing for you, but you can certainly take some steps to help the time and the pain pass more quickly. Borrow my RP^2R pain management process... Relax. Pamper. Play. Reflect. Or better yet, develop your own unique process to help get through those tough moments. Focus on taking baby steps throughout each day to feel better. Don't spend time worrying about the rest of your life right now. Think about getting through the next hour. You don't have to deal with the entire rest of your life right this minute. It's perfectly fine to stop and take extra special care of yourself while you go through the painful process of the passage of time. Don't fall into the trap of becoming something you are not to avoid dealing with the pain. Your relationship has much better odds of survival if you find someone who wants similar things. Stay true to yourself and be flexible as you grow and change throughout your future. Enjoy the time you have alone... use it to honestly get to know yourself. Enjoy the time you have with your partner... use it to experience fabulous things together. Time doesn't have to be the thing that slips away. Time can be your advantage... but only if you allow it to be!

Chapter 12

"The Wrap"

So here I am, in October 2001, at what I hope is the end of my relationship hell. I find myself excited and energized by the potential of my future. I am focused on insuring that I learn and grow from my past experiences. All ten of these lessons will be very important for success in my future relationships. I have learned the hard way that men and women are different, that I'm a high maintenance woman, and that I need to live in the reality, not the fantasy. I've learned to beware of the Master of Deception, that sex does not equal love, and that communication is a big key to relationship success. I've struggled to recognize that love doesn't conquer all, that there is no why in love, and that breaking up is hard to do. And through it all, time has been like a four-letter word!

I hope you found some things in this book helpful. I hope you will now be better able to avoid the mistakes I have made. I hope you discovered some new tools to try in your current and future relationships. At the very least, I hope this book sparked your desire to think about your relationships and what's really important to you. I'm thankful that I've developed a perspective that is much more balanced. I know that actually putting my lessons into action in my next relationship will be far more challenging than just recognizing them and putting them on paper. But understanding what I need to do differently is the first step! I'm confident I'll be able to use these experiences to be more flexible in how I approach my future relationships. Remember that you are the only one who can make the right decisions about what will work for you!

In this book, we started construction on a relationship house. We built a foundation of emotional and physical intimacy. Then we built a solid frame with a strong communication process. Finally, we constructed our walls of trust. Let's finish out this house, because I think there a few additional elements that will help you build a relationship that can weather any storm. Let's start with a roof of self-discipline. Self-discipline can provide you with two things. The first is an ability to stay relentlessly focused on all the things that are important for your relationship. Self-discipline is what you must use to implement any of the lessons you might have taken from this book. It will be the thing that helps you remember to pay attention to your relationship. The second benefit of self-discipline is the strength it will give you to ward off temptation. Life is full of temptations of all kinds that can wreak havoc on your relationship. Self-discipline is what you must have to just say, "No!" to those temptations, whether they be sexual, financial, whatever. Self-discipline is what reminds you that you already have something worth saying "no" to protect. It will enable you to keep all those temptations out of your house. The electricity in our relationship house will come from doing activities together. Whatever you like to do, be it dinner, dancing, golf, travel, or bowling, your relationship will get a charge from each activity you enjoy together. So be sure to spend enough time doing fun things together to keep the generator running. Finally, I suggest we build our relationship house out of rubber. Flexibility is key to successfully withstanding the test of time. You'll have to be able to stretch to endure the changes you and your partner will experience throughout life. It will be a great benefit to allow life's little challenges to bounce off your relationship house, rather than to put holes in it. Rubber will also keep you grounded in case your relationship should indeed take a heavy electrical shock! And despite it's flexibility, rubber can actually be as strong as steel. For your relationship to go the distance, you will certainly need a house built from a virtually indestructible material!

Folks, I now have a fundamental belief that the potential for relationship success is completely within our control. If you choose a person who is a good match for your personality core, and manage to find that personality match with some big time chemistry, success is yours for the taking. Sincerely, when you start with the right mix, the rest is all about process. And your relationship process is completely under your control. I think the biggest challenge is finding a person who is a strong match . . . perhaps that's why the theory of the "one" is so prevalent. Honestly, half the battle is just knowing what you are looking for. Be patient and take enough time on the front end to insure you've got the right match. And don't settle for less than you need to go the distance! The ultimate relationship can absolutely be yours if you are willing to take the risk to find it and put the effort into maintaining it! I wish you luck and absolute happiness!

b.

Beth Elias is a successful marketing executive and an accomplished public speaker. She is also both a former Dallas Cowboys Cheerleader and a Dallas Mavericks Dancer. In this book, Beth openly shares her tumultuous relationship experiences in a direct yet lighthearted tone. Readers will both relate to and remember her valuable relationship lessons. Beth holds both bachelor's and master's degrees in marketing.

Printed in the United States
867700002B